GET YOUR LIFE TOGETHER

Also by Pat Boone:

The Honeymoon Is Over
A Miracle a Day Keeps the Devil Away
My Brothers Keeper?
Twixt Twelve & Twenty

GET YOUR LIFE TOGETHER

PAT BOONE

Dale Books

New York

Cover photography by Dan O'Neill

Scripture quotations *are based* on the King James Version
of the Bible.

Also quoted, The Living Bible Paraphrased (Tyndale House
Publishers, Wheaton, Illinois, 1971). Used by permission.

Appreciation is expressed to the publishers for permission
to use material from the following books:
1. Pat Boone, *A New Song*. Creation House Inc.,
   Carol Stream, Ill., 1970.
2. Shirley Boone, *One Woman's Liberation*. Creation House
   Inc., Carol Stream, Ill., 1972.
3. Pat Boone, *A Miracle a Day Keeps the Devil Away*.
   Fleming H. Revell, Old Tappan, N.J., 1974.
4. Pat Boone, *Joy—A Homosexual's Search for Fulfillment*.
   Creation House Inc., Carol Stream, Ill., 1974.

Published by Dale Books, Inc., 380 Lexington Ave.,
New York, N.Y. 10017

TABLE OF CONTENTS

Part One   Introduction 5
1. Does Anybody Need a Friend 11

Part Two   Prayer
1. What Is Prayer, Anyway? 19

Part Three   When Darkness Overwhelms
1. Does God Really Heal? 29
2. The Threshold of Despair 32
3. The Depths of Depression 38
4. The Valley of the Shadow 42

Part Four   On the Lighter Side
1. Overcoming Fear 51
2. The Mouse and I 58
3. Why I Became a Jew 63
4. God on the Night Shift 71

Part Five   The Fractured Family
1. How Parents Help Teenagers Deal with
   Sex Temptations 77
2. A Fallen Woman—Age Seventeen 92
3. Sex Problems in Marriage 99
4. Abortion 103

Part Six   The Devil's Cauldron
1. Witchcraft and Satanism 113
2. That Demon—Rum 119
3. Drug Addiction 124
4. Gay and Happy Aren't the Same 128
5. Fat, Fear, and Faith 134
6. A Cure for Television 141
7. Can We Win Against Pornography? 146

Part Seven   A Glimpse at the Future
1. Pat's Letter to a Noted Astrologer on
   Astrology 155

Part Six The Devil's Cauldron
1. Witchcraft and Satanism 113
2. That Demon—Rum 119
3. Drug Addiction 124
4. Gay and Happy Aren't the Same 128
5. Fat, Fear, and Faith 134
6. A Cure for Television 141
7. Can We Win Against Pornography? 146

Part Seven A Glimpse at the Future
1. Pat's Letter to a Noted Astrologer on Astrology 155

PART ONE: INTRODUCTION

1. Does Anybody Need a Friend?

INTRODUCTION

Lots of things are coming apart at the seams these days.

Big businesses, brand new cars, some democratic institutions, whole governments, the ecology, old-fashioned morality, the world's balance of power—and lots of lives.

Almost 50 percent of America's marriages are ending in divorce. Suicide is on an upward spiral, even among high school and *junior* high kids. Alcoholism, drug addiction and venereal disease are all at epidemic proportions. Violence and open criminality are seeping into every neighborhood. Economic earthquakes are snuffing out millions of jobs, while runaway inflation is deflating savings accounts and insurance benefits. Kids from every economic and social level are dropping out of churches, schools and jobs and they're thumbing rides on freeways to *any*where, *no*where. Many of them are drifting into militant underground organizations, homosexuality or occult activity. Mystic and psychic "religions" are flourishing while churches are dwindling—and the hospitals and psychiatrists' offices are packed to the rafters!

Would you say we've got a few problems?

I would; and I can add a few of my own!

";What?" somebody says, *"You've* got problems? The All-American boy, Joe College, the guy with the gold records and all the kids, the TV and movie star, Mr. Religious with the pretty wife and a big home in Beverly Hills? *You've* got *problems?"*

Yep, big ones. And I've been painfully frank about the crises in my life, talking openly about them on TV, radio and in my own spiritual autobiography, *A New Song*.[1] A soured marriage, disintegrating financial problems—finally facing divorce, bankruptcy and ridicule. Shirley has also poured out her heart in a best-selling book, *One Woman's Liberation*,[2] revealing that our mounting problems brought her to the very brink of emotional and physical breakdown.

But, thank God, the story didn't end there!

Our problems had answers!

We desperately needed miracles, in every area of our lives, and they happened—as we individually turned ourselves back to the Maker of Miracles. One by one, occasionally just in the nick of time, each of our problems was solved, often in a gloriously supernatural way. And life became a daily adventure, prompting another book *A Miracle a Day Keeps the Devil Away*.[3]

Our whole family was so happy that we wanted to share our excitement with others. We went on TV programs, all the talk shows; wrote articles and books; began recording; performing; traveling together and shouting for the world to hear. "Hey, you folks with all the problems! You don't have to keep on being victims, statistics, and casualties! There *are* answers. You *can* win. You can have your *own* daily miracles! Marriage can work, families can be terrifically successful, finances and careers can stabilize, bodies and emotions can be healed. And *it's as simple as inviting God to live at your house and allowing Him to be your guide and partner!* It's not a 'religion'—it's a Person! And His name is Jesus."

[1] Pat Boone, *A New Song*. Creation House Inc., Carol Stream, Ill., 1970.

[2] Shirley Boone, *One Woman's Liberation*. Creation House Inc., Carol Stream, Ill., 1972.

[3] Pat Boone, *A Miracle a Day Keeps the Devil Away*. Fleming H. Revell, Old Tappan, N.J., 1974.

People heard us. And they responded.

The letters began pouring in from people with similar problems—and worse. Some of the most horrible, hopeless and frightening situations imaginable cascaded onto my desk. Human problems of terrible magnitude stacked up there, from real folks who were desperate for God's answers, *any* answers, and NOW!

Though I was busy with my career, family and other activities, I couldn't ignore those letters. I've never been able to do that.

So Shirley and I (and sometimes our daughters) burrowed through our Bibles, sought the expert advice of professionals, and prayed a lot. We answered the letters and earnestly offered the spiritual prescriptions we'd found. . . .

And they worked!

Letters were coming back now, but vastly different ones. These were filled with excitement and good news and personal miracles, hopeless situations reversed, personalities transformed, marriages glued back together and failures turned into triumphs!

God, the loving Creator, was touching other people's lives, just as He had ours. It was deeply moving.

He gave us answers that worked.

Photoplay magazine, the premier publication of the movie/TV world, offered me space every month to share some of this excitement with its readers, and the response has been tremendous. In beauty parlors, bus stations, drugstores and supermarkets, in all kinds of "unreligious" places, folks were reading about real human problems with real practical and documented *answers*. And increasingly, the readers have dared to try our "spiritual prescriptions" themselves—and the miracles have come!

And now, this book.

My family and I still want to spread the news that *God is interested* in you! He's not nearly as concerned with which religion you're part of as He is with *you*, your problems, your dreams—and your life. He loves you, cares about you, and He wants to be involved with you in every part of your life. He desires a Father-child relationship with you.

Jesus has made this possible, and has shown us how it works.

And friend, it *does work!*

Each of the chapters in this book deals with a real situation, and the answers and advice we've found in the Manufacturer's Handbook, the Bible. Much of this priceless information has been on our bookshelves and under our noses for thousands of years, but it's as timely and practical as the latest electronic computer readout. God doesn't change, and neither do people. Gadgets and "things" may fool us into thinking our problems are different, but they're not.

In an unbroken line, all the way back to Eden, people and their basic needs have been just the same. From the very beginning, a loving Father-God has been waiting to supply those needs to anybody who would ask Him, and be willing to try life *His* way.

Through Abraham, Moses, Elijah, David—and Jesus, His firstborn Son—He's been saying, "Let Me help you get your life together—"

And He means it.

The answers in these pages, most of them published before in the *Photoplay* articles, are not my own. At least, I've tried to keep myself and my personal opinions in the background and just pass along what I've found in the Bible. They've worked for us, and as you'll see, for lots of other folks like you. Wherever necessary, I've changed names, but the situations and their solutions are real, twentieth-century facts.

Right now, I'll share with you a letter that reflects the most common basic problem of all—the universal need for a friend.

I'm starting with this one because I feel it underlies all the other breakdowns in the human condition. The answer is so simple that you may reject it at first.

But please read on. After you've shared with me some of the heartbreak and victory of later chapters, you may find that this first example makes pretty good sense after all.

You might even want to try the answer yourself—whatever your problems may be.

I'll guarantee you one thing.

This Friend, if you'll let Him, will get your life together.

1. DOES ANYBODY NEED A FRIEND?

Dear Pat:

Sometimes I think I'm the loneliest person in the world. I have a good paying job, although it's dull. I live away from my family—we always argued about everything anyway—and I feel I have no real friends. Oh, I know some people, and I do go to church sometimes, and nobody is really mean to me—it all seems so phony! I just feel I don't really have one true friend in the world, somebody that really cares about me or would be disappointed if I were to die.

Thinking about it gets me very depressed. How in this world does a person find a real friend? I hope you can help me.

Jonell Jacobs

Dear Jonell:

I've had so many letters like this one. I suppose most entertainers have, but since my articles began in *Photoplay*, I've had a real avalanche of mail from just plain old lonely people. We all *do* need friends, and most of all we need the one Friend who said, "Greater love has no man than this, that He lay down His life for His friends." Jesus said that, and Jesus did just that, for you and me.

Sensing the universal loneliness and the desperate need we all have for friends, I wrote what I call "Personal Message From Pat Boone." I had this printed with a picture on the front, and a signature on the back, and have given away over 10,000 in the last couple of years to people I meet in public places. I've been asked for autographs everywhere I've gone for the last 20 years, and it seemed such a ridiculous waste of time, I decided if I was going to give an autograph, it should be attached to something worth keeping. Since the subject is friends, I offer this personal statement to you in its entirety. I hope you will accept it as if I had just handed it to you in person.

Dear Friend . . .

That's a beautiful word, isn't it?—"Friend." When it's used properly, the word says so much. Not many of us have a lot of *real* friends. I want you to know my friend, Jesus. He wants to be your friend, too. Does it sound irreverent to refer to Jesus as *my friend?* It shouldn't. Jesus said Himself, "Greater love has no man than this, that a man lay down his life for his friend" (see John 15:13). And He did just that. He did it for me, and He did it for you.

He actually gave His life so that you and He could be friends, in the most intimate, personal way. He actually said, "Look! I have been standing at the door and I am constantly knocking. If anyone hears me calling him and opens the door, I will come in and fellowship with Him and he with me" (Revelation 3:20).

What else could anyone do, or say, to prove his willing friendship?

"Well, that sounds nice," you may say, "but I just don't need Jesus as my friend. I'm doing fine."

Are you?

You have all the answers, you know what life is all about? You're realizing your full potential as a human being? Your relationships with other people are everything you want them to be? You know no fears—no doubts? You understand the incredibly complex problems that confront us all, with the rising tensions and frustrations and dangers, and feel adequate to cope with them—alone?

Please . . . don't kid yourself.

Every human being alive today needs Jesus as his friend!

You've heard the funny story about the psychiatrist who says to his mousy patient, "Inferiority complex? Let's face it—you *are* inferior!"

We keep hearing about "guilt complexes"; well, let's face it—we are guilty! The Bible says, "Yes, all have sinned; all fall short of God's glorious ideal" (Romans 3:23) and the sentence is eternal separation from God *and* death (Romans 6:23). Deny it, hide it, try to "live with it," reject it if you will. You might as well reject the law of gravity.

By your own actions, you've been found guilty—and sentenced to death!

"Yet now God declares us 'not guilty' of offending him if we trust in Jesus Christ, who in his kindness freely takes away our sins. For God sent Christ Jesus to take the punishment for our sins and to end all God's anger against us" (Romans 3:24, 25).

And you don't need Him?

You think you can make it through this life, and face God someday—alone? You don't need the happiness, the confidences, the daily thrill of a personal relationship with the living God?

"Okay, okay," I hear you say, "I'll admit it sounds good; I do need something better in my life. But how do I know when I've got it?"

Jesus says in John 14, "I am the way, I am the truth, I am the life; no one comes to the Father, but by me!" And in Revelation 3, "If anyone hears me calling him and opens the door, I will come in!"

But we can't see Jesus; how do we know He's come in?

Can you see electricity? Can you see X-rays? No. But when you come in contact with electric current, you feel its reality! And when you're exposed to the X-ray machine, you see the results!

So it is with Jesus. We don't see Him, because He demands faith. Yet, when you truly open the door of your life to Him, yield your will to His, you'll begin to feel the reality of His presence. He will make His intimate friendship with you known, as you honestly seek it. And the visible results will be obvious to you and to all who know you, because they'll see Him in you! You can ask Him to supply your specific needs, satisfy your deepest longings—and when you start seeing and feeling the answers to your prayers, the excitement of this previous relationship will bubble over; you won't be able to hide it! I know!

See, friend, we think backward; we think of ourselves as human bodies who have souls. That's wrong. We are souls, and we have bodies! And Jesus comes in to dwell with our souls, our eternal selves, by the power of His Holy Spirit. (Read 1 John 4:13.) He's not bound by physical limits.

But you have to invite Him—you have to really want Him as your friend. And tell Him that you do.

Why don't you do that right now?

Wherever you're sitting—standing—right now; as you read this, if you don't know Jesus as your friend, your intimate Lord and companion, talk to Him—as you do to any friend, and tell Him you need Him.

Talk to Him about your needs, your failures, your weaknesses, and your sins. Ask Him to take them away, to forgive you. He will! (Read I John 1:9.) Ask Him to live with you from now on, in your heart and soul. He will!

Believe it! Believing is a matter of choice, of will, of your personal determination. And God demands it! He calls it FAITH (Hebrews 11:6).

But thank God, faith isn't just grit and will power; the Bible says that "faith comes by hearing the good news, and the word of God" (Romans 10:17). Get yourself a New Testament, perhaps the Living New Testament—and get acquainted with the truest, strongest, most precious Friend you'll ever have—JESUS!

It's vital that you read what Jesus did and said while He walked the earth; you need to know how He treated people, what He saw as important, what moved Him to tears and great joy, and—most important of all—what He expects of you as His friend, and what He promises you, right here and now, because of your relationship to Him!

The Son of God, Jesus, promises you a more exciting, fulfilling, confident, vibrant life than you can imagine—read it for yourself!

And—when **you** hear Him, in His Word, telling you to do something, OBEY Him! His laws are for our good, and obedience brings rich blessings! Try Him! Let Him prove it to you.

For example, when you hear Him say, "He that believeth and is baptized shall be saved"—*obey Him* (Mark 16:16). Be baptized! Why? Because Jesus did it; He asked you to; and because obedience brings forgiveness, salvation, and eternal blessing (Acts 2:38).

How can I describe the cleansing beauty of that symbolic death, burial and resurrection? You have to experience it for yourself—with Jesus, and because of Jesus (1 Peter 3:21).

That's the fantastic beauty of this whole thing, this friendship with Jesus! It's impossible to describe to others, because it's so personal, so intimate, so individual! It's between you and your Friend, Jesus.

Soon you'll find yourself devouring His Word, finding the twentieth century practicality, the wonder and excitement of being in tune with the power that shaped our universe! You'll know the fantastic realization that eternity has begun for you already! The urgency of problems will dissolve into confident assurance based on Romans 8:28 (Read it!).

And you'll be sharing this with others—you can't help it! You'll be bringing your friends to meet OUR Friend, Jesus. Be sure to ask God to lead you into a Bible-believing, Jesus-honoring church. He'll do it, because He knows we need the fellowship and encouragement of other believers all the time.

God bless you——FRIEND.

PART TWO: PRAYER
1. What Is Prayer, Anyway?

1. WHAT IS PRAYER, ANYWAY?

Dear Pat Boone:

I've been reading your articles in *Photoplay*, and really enjoy them. I wish I had the kind of faith you seem to have. I've got lots of problems, which I won't go into now, but I really wonder if God hears everybody pray, the way you say. You keep telling people with problems that they should pray, and I'm not really sure I know how to.

What is prayer, anyway?

Logan

Dear Logan:

I'm really glad you asked that question. It is really top priority—so much depends on the answer. I guess I assume that most people know how to pray, and really that's too big an assumption. Reflecting on how to answer you, I've just realized it took me a long time to learn how to pray. And I don't think I've ever been asked for a definition. So here goes.

Prayer is conversation with God.

Think about that a minute before you reject it. I know most people don't think of prayer as "conversation," and certainly not *"with* God." Most folks who pray simply talk to the air, with their eyes squinted closed, usually with heads bowed, and in subdued voices. I have no doubt that God hears that kind of prayer, but from my study in the Bible, and my own experience, I know He means for us to experience more freedom and two-way communication than that.

It's funny that little children seem to sense what prayer is supposed to be better than adults. When Cherry was just three or so, Shirley knelt with her and her two little sisters for a good-night prayer. It was Cherry's night to lead the prayer (we've always taken turns), and in her little Doctor Denton's, she asked God to bless everybody we knew—and then stopped. While Shirley and the others kept their heads bowed and wondered what was happening, several minutes went by in silence. Finally, Cherry spoke again, "God, will you speak a little louder?—I can't quite hear you!"

Shirley and I wondered about that for a long time.

Our little three-year-old seemed to expect to *hear* the voice of God in response to her prayers. And it's taken me a long time to find out that she was right. God *does* respond to our prayers, and wants us to learn to recognize His answers; in fact, Jesus specifically said, "My sheep *hear My voice.*"

The Bible says that God doesn't change, and throughout that very Book, from cover to cover, we see examples of individuals speaking to God, and hearing His answer in return! Quite often, we see them getting specific direction, sometimes approval, sometimes correction and chastisement—but unmistakably hearing the voice of God Himself! Adam and Abraham and Moses and Joshua and Ezekiel and Isaiah—and Jesus—all knew that prayer is to be a two-way street. So where have we lost it?

In the first place, we don't *expect* to hear anything, so we don't *listen.* Most of us are not even sure that God *hears* us, to begin with. And then, we've learned such a ritualistic, unnatural and affected way of praying, that it's very hard for us to spend much time at it. Too many of us approach God as if we were asking for a job we knew we weren't qualified for, or even like little school children, fearfully asking the principal for permission to leave school early. And yet God, through the whole Bible, has demonstrated over and over that He wants to be involved with us in our daily lives, and that He will work with us on an intimate basis, if we'll let Him.

Jesus, as always, is the perfect example. He kept saying, "If you've seen Me, you've seen the Father." In other words, if you'll watch the way I do things, you'll know how God wants to relate to you. In Luke 11, when Jesus' disciples specifically asked Him to teach them to pray, He gave them the most practical and simple example. We now call it "The Lord's Prayer." If you'll look at that again, you'll see that it *is* conversation with God. Jesus got right down to business with His Father, acknowledged His greatness, and then spelled out the three or four basic things that He was interested in. And with hardly a breath, He went right on to other teachings.

Simple? Yes, and basic, and profound. And it works!

The Bible says that David was a man after God's own heart. And the book of Psalms is a collection of 150 of David's prayers. If you really want to know how to pray, and if you really want to know how to hear the voice of God, you can follow David's example. Read the Psalms, see how he rejoiced to be in God's presence, see how specific and intimate and honest He was—and begin to do the same thing.

Logan, be honest—be child-like—be real.

Paul, the mighty Jewish scholar, recognized these things and promised to those who had become the sons of God (the Messiah, Jesus, made this possible) that God gives us the "Spirit of adoption" who authorizes us to cry "Abba, Father." That Hebrew word, *Abba*, means "Daddy." It's a very intimate expression that children used toward their fathers in Paul's day, and Jewish kids still do. In Romans 8 and Galatians 4, Paul makes quite plain that those who have accepted God's permanent offering for sin, His only Son, have the right to speak to Him as their beloved Daddy. Doesn't this imply a conversational, though respectful and reverent, approach?

David admonishes in the Hundredth Psalm, "Enter into his gates with thanksgiving, and into his courts with praise." I used to think that these were "things" you brought with you; I realize now they are the *doors* through which you enter.

You actually enter into the gates of God as you give Him thanks.

You enter into His inner court as you praise Him, with your heart and spirit.

First, the gates. Logan, if you'll just get off in a quiet place anywhere, and simply say something like, "Lord, I really thank You that I'm alive, I really thank You that You care about me. I really thank You that I can speak to You this way, and I thank You that You promise to hear me. By the way, I really thank You for my mom and dad, and for my job, and for the good food I had yesterday. While we're at it, I'm thankful for this body, my brain, and for You Word." I'll guarantee you that you will soon know you have entered the presence of God, and that He is hearing you.

This is the way you enter the gates of God. But what about praise? How is it that you enter into the very inner court, the holy of holies of the Lord Himself? Praise is an avenue of communication that most adults have completely forgotten; but Jesus said in Matthew 21, "out of the mouths of babes and nursing infants *God has perfect praise.*"

You can't get better than "perfect," can you? And Jesus, quoting David in the eighth Psalm says that nursing infants praise God perfectly. How? Well, that stumped me, until I remembered what it was like when my four girls were nursing infants. I remembered looking over the edge of the crib, and I remember my daughter's reaction when she saw her daddy. She usually responded enthusiastically, wiggling and reaching up to me and talking a mile a minute—even though she hadn't learned how! She was so delighted to see me that she was spontaneously calling me, in every way she could, "Daddy, I love you. Daddy, please pick me up. Daddy, I'm so happy to see you—Daddy, I need you. Daddy, I'm wet—or hungry. Daddy, please pick your daughter up." And, Logan, you know something, I *knew* what she was saying, even though I didn't understand all her words. Because she was my daughter, and I loved her, and I knew beyond a doubt that she loved me. And even today, though my daughters are 18, 19, 20, and 21, it's still the same; the fastest way to get my attention is for one of my daughters to say, "Daddy, I love you."

That's praise, and no father—especially our heavenly Father—can resist it. Logan, my whole life changed when I began to learn to praise the Lord. Like David, I discovered that God delights in our praise, and responds! He spoke through the writer James and said in the fourth chapter, "Draw near to God and *He will draw near to you.*" That's God's promise; and He keeps His promises!

I recently recorded an album, "Songs from the Inner Court," in which I sing love songs to the King, and praise Him with my heart, my mind and my spirit. It was an intense worship experience for me, and I really believe that those who hear it are drawn into the inner court with me. I'd really recommend it to you, and if you're interested, write me and I'll see that you get it.

I know it sounds impossible for God to hear all our prayers, and to be so close that we can simply speak, and know that He hears. But the prophet Isaiah said long ago, "Therefore the Lord Himself shall give you a sign; behold, a virgin shall conceive, and bear a son, and shall call His name Emmanuel" (Isaiah 7:24). You know what Emmanuel means?—"God with us." And Jesus said in Matthew 28:20, just before He ascended into Heaven, "Lo, *I am with you always,* even to the end of the world."

I know I always come running when one of my children calls out to me; and God is a much better father than I am.

And what should a person pray about? Anything! And I mean—*anything!* In Mark 11:24, Matthew 6:5-8, and First John 3:22, as well as James 4:2-3, the Lord insists that we should ask for anything; that He knows what we have need of before we ask; and that we have not, because we *ask* not. But there is a catch, of course. The Bible clearly says that we must ask *in faith;* forgiving others as we have been forgiven;

in Jesus' name; and in line with God's will for us as He has revealed it in His Word.

But those conditions don't limit our right to pray; they only limit the kind of answers that we receive. James adds, "You ask and receive *not*, because you ask amiss, that you might consume it upon your own lusts (or pleasures)."

Again, as a father, though I want to give my children the things that will make them happy, and the things they want—because I love them—I must sometimes say "no," or "wait." Our Father God won't usually grant our requests, if they would harm us, and He knows that far better than we do. There are times revealed in the Bible when David and Hezekiah and Moses actually caused him to change His mind through their prayers, but it didn't always work out for their good. The people of Israel begged for a king, and though God didn't want to give them a king because it was not for their best, He relented and set up Saul and David and Solomon, but the kingly office degenerated, and there were many more bad kings than good—and eventually the corrupt kings brought about Israel's slavery.

Father does know best!

And the Father says to His children, "Put me in remembrance; let us argue our case *together*, state your cause, that you may be proved right" (Isaiah 43:26). Could He make it any more plain? He *is* a loving Father, a wonderful provider, and He's willing to listen to our arguments, and to reason with us, and gently lead us into His own will, which will fulfill and complete us in every way. What more could we ask?

But one last reality. The Bible also says clearly that we don't know how to pray as we should. We really don't know what to ask for, what will make us happy in the long run, or how to pray for other people, no matter how much we love them. But God's got even that covered! In Romans 8, He promises that "the Spirit Himself intercedes for us with groanings too deep for words. And He who searches the hearts knows what the mind of the spirit is, because He (Jesus) intercedes for the saints (that's you and me) *according to the will of God.*"

Isn't that fantastic? God Himself, by the Holy Spirit, will actually help us with our praying, if we let Him and ask Him to.

So, Logan, that's my final bit of advice. Ask the Holy Spirit to teach you how to pray, to help you pray, and to pray with and for you to our loving Father. He's promised to do it, so take Him up on it. Jump in and get into the Word. Find out more and more what His will is for you, and rejoice with me that His will is always for our good (Romans 8:28).

Begin and end your prayers telling the Father that you love Him. Mean it with all your heart, and you'll find that "the love of God is shed abroad in our hearts by the Holy Spirit, who is given to us" (Romans 5:5). You'll find that your ability to love grows and grows, that your understanding of the Word grows, and that your ability to pray will greatly increase. And with that ability, there will come a joy and a strength and a maturity and a wisdom beyond your fondest imagination.

Prayer *does* begin and end with love—because God *is* love.

Your brother in Jesus,
PAT

PART THREE:
WHEN DARKNESS OVERWHELMS

1. Does God Really Heal?
2. The Threshold of Despair
3. The Depths of Depression
4. The Valley of the Shadow

1. DOES GOD REALLY HEAL?

Dear Mr. Boone:

In a recent "talk program" on TV you mentioned your book, *A New Song*, and I got it to send to a friend of mine who has been having problems with "modern morality" ideas. I read it before mailing it, and was impressed with your clear-cut faith in the miracle of healing. I grew up with a good Christian background, and several times "went forward" in camp-meeting revivals, seeking a conversion like Saul's on the road to Damascus—without apparent results. I finally decided I had to settle for just putting my feet in the Way, and accepted Major Farrington's "If Jesus Christ is a man, and only a man, I swear, then of all mankind will I cleave to him—I will follow him everywhere."

Two years ago we took into our home a grandson whose parents were advised his birth defects from "open spine" were such that he would never be even close to normal, mentally or physically, and he should be placed in a state institution. Fortunately, there were no openings at the time, and since his parents already had three small children at home to care for, we took him until an opening should occur. We have since witnessed the miracle of his mind unfolding, through wonderful school programs and teachers here. He has begun speaking, and through the Crippled Children's Services and the State Mental Hygiene program, his "crossed eyes" have been corrected. His twisted legs are now straight enough to allow the use of crutches. He still has some emotional problems, and the problem of lack of control of bowels and bladder, so he is a full-time job for his grandpa and me, but he is a charming little fellow and has so much potential. It grieves us that his parents have not fully opened their hearts and lives again to him. They live 200 miles from us, and he sees them all too infrequently. There are no such schools or programs for him in their city.

This morning I awakened with the thought that I would like to hunt through the New Testament in modern language which I purchased after reading your book, to see what words were used about Christ's feeling "virtue is gone out of me" when the woman touched his garment. I turned on TV to Oral Roberts' program, and he quoted the incident, and he offered his book, *The Healing Scriptures*, in which there is a chapter on the healing of children. Is God nudging me to believe this little 5½-year-old of ours can be healed, whose feet are "impotent from his mother's womb," even as the man Peter healed? We have friends who, when they first saw our lad, said, "You know he can be healed if you have faith to believe." I felt then that this would be asking too much—that we were seeing miracles happening through doctors, surgeons and teachers, and this is all we should ask for. But my husband is 68 and I am 67 and we know we cannot see this child to adulthood, and there is ill-will brewing between my husband and son which I have feared would spoil the child's chances of an eventual return to his parents, so now I can only pray, "Lord, I believe. Help thou mine unbelief," and ask for your advice and prayers.

Sincerely,
Mrs. John Taylor

Dear Sister:

I appreciated your letter and was really warmed by the spirit of it. God bless you and your husband, and especially you and your grandson. I'm sure He loves that little boy, and has already been working in his life through you.

I do feel, Mrs. Taylor, that the Lord has the power and the will to bring your grandson to normalcy. As I was looking for a certain Scripture to refer you to, my Bible opened to

Luke 4, beginning with verse 17 and continuing to verse 27. I believe this relates to John 9:1, where the disciples asked Jesus who it was who sinned that this child should be born blind? Jesus told them the answer was: "Neither; it was in order that the works of God might be displayed in him." In both of these Scriptures Jesus underlines the idea that not all are healed of their diseases, but God does heal many and always to the glory of His Son, Jesus. In Matthew 8:1-3 and Luke 5:13 I believe that Jesus indicates His willingness that all should be healed, but in John 5:39 He tells us that many searched the Scriptures thinking that eternal life was in the Scriptures—and indeed it is, but only as they bring people to the person of Jesus Himself.

I say all of that in leading up to this; the more you tenderly minister to your grandson and the more you ask Jesus Himself to touch him and to inhabit him and to truly make your grandson's flesh His own, the more God will be encouraged to use your grandson to manifest the glory of Jesus. I really would encourage your grandson, too, to talk to Jesus and speak His name and literally "come to Him." Nothing is impossible with God, and though we have to submit our will to His, He encourages us to ask anything in His name and then to believe that we receive it. Oral Roberts has another book, a short one, entitled *Seven Reasons I Know You Can Be Healed.* I would encourage you to send for that, Oral Roberts, Tulsa, Oklahoma 74105. He is a wonderful man and God has given him a great ministry. Also, may I encourage you to pray for your son and daughter and to continually bathe them in the love of Jesus and to rebuke any work of Satan in their lives or in yours so that the Lord can be completely free to work His will. If Satan could influence Peter right in the presence of Jesus, enough so that Jesus had to say "get thee behind me, Satan," then we have to beware of his influence in our lives, too.

God bless you all, and let me know the good news.

Yours in Him,
PAT BOONE

2. THE THRESHOLD OF DESPAIR

Dear Mr. Boone:

I don't know if you will help me, but I thought I'd try. All you can do is say no.

Do you know what cystic fibrosis is? My oldest son has been in a therapy hospital with that disease since he was 5 months old, and they have no idea if he'll ever be well enough to come home. If he does come home we'll have to have a mist tent for him to sleep in. Cystic fibrosis is a fatal lung disease, and what's even worse is that if I have another child I take a big chance that the new baby could have it too, because my husband and I are both carriers.

The problem is that we live 20 miles from my son's hospital. We're at least two months behind in payments on everything we owe, and can't afford to drive to see him. We have to live with my husband's mother because of our lack of money, and the bills are due again. We haven't seen our son for over a month, and if things keep going the way they are, we won't be able to get him home for his birthday.

Our other son is in the hospital for tests, and if they come out positive he'll have to live in the hospital, too.

We have a bank note of $200, we owe on a pick-up truck for $650, two credit charges equal almost $300, and there is a loan for $400. The hospital bill for our second son (who was born prematurely) is $1500. The total is over three thousand dollars.

That's about all my husband makes in a year. And there are food, clothes, and other doctor bills, repairs on our truck and much more. Could you help me? I'm so discouraged with the bills and not being able to get our son for the weekend, I don't know what I'll do. I pray you'll help. Please answer if you don't or can't help. I just need to know you got my letter.

Thank you,
Mary

(This is one of the hardest letters I've ever had to answer. As you can see, it's utterly heartbreaking and hopeless, humanly speaking. But that's just humanly speaking. If all I had were human answers for people's problems, I wouldn't try to answer these letters or write monthly articles in *Photoplay*. Fortunately for all of us, God has answers to every problem that *work!* Because of the economic "squeeze" we're all experiencing, because of mounting unemployment, because we're all concerned about poverty and its victims, and because every entertainer in show business gets heartbreaking letters like this—I really prayed about the answer that I wrote to Mary. I offer it to you now. God says it will work!)

Dear Mary:

Your letter tears me to pieces.

My first reaction is to want to pick up the phone, call my accountant, and ask him if we can mail you the money you need. Two things stop me. One is that this wouldn't solve your long-range problems; so there must be a better answer than that. And the other is that I get hundreds of letters like this every year—and if I obeyed my first impulse (to call my accountant) everytime, I would soon be writing a letter like yours to someone else.

So with a prayer for guidance, I say to you what the apostle Peter said to the man who had been lame from birth:

"The lame man looked at them eagerly, expecting a gift. But Peter said, 'We don't have any money for you! But I'll give you something else! I command you in the name of

Jesus Christ of Nazareth, *walk!'* Then Peter took the lame man by the hand and pulled him to his feet. And as he did, the man's feet and ankle bones were healed and strengthened so that he came up with a leap, stood there a moment, and began walking! Then, walking, leaping, and praising God, he went into the temple with them!" (Acts 3, The Living Bible).

Mary, please follow me closely.

In this true account, Peter and John were confronted with a very human need. They knew that money was not the answer (though that's what the lame man was asking for). They saw that a miracle of God was called for, and that this lame man had the faith to expect a miracle. So together they called on God, and the miracle that he needed *happened*. And when his deepest needs were met, the lame man knew that *God* had touched him, and he ran around praising *Him*.

I feel sure that yours is a similar situation.

I know that your human needs are very great, both physically and financially. And the very *fact that you have written me for help* indicates that you're not fully believing God to meet your needs. In fact, though you may have a deep and real faith, you don't mention Him anywhere in your letter.

So I'm going to offer you a spiritual prescription, which—if you will use it in faith—will lead to the solution of *all* your problems. I'll make it brief and to the point.

First, if you haven't already done it, give yourself wholeheartedly into God's hands, receiving Jesus as your Saviour. Each member of your family should do this, and you will immediately become eligible for this promise: *My God shall supply all your needs according to His riches in glory by Christ Jesus* (Philippians 4:19).

Second, get a Bible (if you don't have one I'll send it to you) and begin to read the words of Jesus Himself, and start talking to Him constantly, asking Him to help you understand those words and put them into practice in your life. He'll do it!

Third, a real test of faith! But I personally guarantee it will work (only because it's backed up by the Bank of Heaven). Start *giving a tenth of every dollar you earn to God*—and watch how He multiplies it back to you. Listen to His promise: "Honor the Lord with thy substance, and with the firstfruits of all thine increase; so shall thy barns be filled with plenty, and thy presses shall burst out with new wine" (Proverbs 3:9-10).

Listen to God's promise again: "Bring ye all the tithes into the storehouse, that there may be meat in mine house, and prove me now herewith, saith the Lord of hosts, if I will not *open you the windows of heaven, and pour you out a blessing, that there shall not be room enough to receive it*" (Malachi 3:10).

Mary, that's not a human bank or government or church speaking—that's God Himself making you a promise! Do you dare to take Him up on it?

Read the next verse in Malachi 3 (verse 11), "And I will rebuke the devourer for your sakes, and he shall not destroy the fruits of your ground." Combine that with what Jesus said in John 10:10, *"The thief* cometh not but for to steal, to kill, and to destroy." Both Malachi and Jesus were speaking of the same person—Satan. Jesus called him a thief and a destroyer, and you've been learning first hand that Jesus was telling the truth, haven't you? It's easy for me to see that Satan has been robbing you and trying to destroy your son. And he'll succeed—unless you call out to the only power in heaven and earth who can really defend you.

Be daring. At this point, you really don't have much to lose, do you? Scrape together every cent that you can possibly give, and put it in your church collection plate, or give it to the Salvation Army, or the nearest orphanage or hospital fund, and pray as you do it, telling the Lord that you're giving it to Him as an *act of faith and confidence in His promises.* Better yet, look around and find somebody who is in at least as bad a situation as you are, and personally give them the money in the name of Jesus. If you possibly can, give 10 percent of the total amount you urgently need right away.

Mary, I know this sounds frightening and impractical, and foolish—from a human standpoint. But we're not looking for human solutions. We're looking for a *miracle!*

And listen to the promise from the very lips of the miracle worker Himself: "For if you give, you will get! Your gift will return to you in full and overflowing measure, pressed down, shaken together to make room for more, and running over. *Whatever measure you use to give—large or small—will be used to measure what is given back to you*" (Luke 6:38).

Jesus promises you that if you give to Him, or to someone else in His name, He will multiply it back to you at a rate faster than inflation can possibly keep up with!

Mary, I know that this may be hard to believe, and even harder to put into practice. There's so much poverty in the world today that it staggers us to think about it. But I earnestly believe that if every individual believed God's words, and acted on them, poverty would cease. Think—if all of us were giving to meet each other's needs, and God were multiplying back to us according to our own giving, human financial problems would soon be solved, wouldn't they? But this has to happen on an individual basis, because that's the way God works with people.

I'd really recommend that you send for a book called *The Laws of Prosperity* by Kenneth Copeland, P.O. Box 3407, Fort Worth, Texas. I believe it's the best book on financial security ever written—at least, since the Bible itself.

One last promise from Jesus Himself, in His great Sermon on the Mount: "So don't worry at all about having enough food and clothing. Why be like the heathen? For they take pride in all these things and are deeply concerned about them. But your heavenly father already knows perfectly well that you need them, and *He will give them to you if you give*

Him first place in your life and live as He wants you to"
(Matthew 6).

So don't be anxious about tomorrow, God will take care
of your tomorrow too. Live one day at a time.

God bless you.
PAT BOONE

3. THE DEPTHS OF DEPRESSION

Dear Pat and Shirley Boone:
    I've read your recent books and felt their profound Christian influence. The emotional conflict in my life at present is so urgent, I hardly know how to tell you.
    Several years ago we lost our son in an accident. There are two children living.
    A few years after that, my husband had a nervous breakdown, and underwent treatment for six weeks. He was prescribed tranquilizers, but often used alcohol instead. Last year his illness, a severe depression, recurred. He is 50 years old.
    At the present he is living in solitary confinement, except for my presence, during most of the days and nights. He was in former days outgoing and ambitious. He refuses professional treatment, but doesn't drink or smoke now.
    He never leaves our home for even a minute, and seems intelligent in thinking processes, but he is deteriorating socially.
    I feel you could know us so much better if I'd write all the interesting details of our family and the faith I've tried to live and maintain. I'm sure, though, that you can read between the lines. . . .
    Please write.

Sincerely,
Mrs. Marsha Jones

Dear Mrs. Jones:
    Your letter has touched our hearts, and we are praying

that our Heavenly Father will minister very specially and specifically to each one in your family, and that He will grant you His peace.

The needs of your husband are deep, and no doubt causing increased stress on you and the family. It would be good if you all could receive good Christian professional counseling, but if Christian counselors are not available in your area, we know that the Holy Spirit can do the work without trained counselors. In fact, one of the names given to our Lord Jesus is "Counselor." Jesus, when He began His ministry right after His personal encounter with Satan, announced exactly what His counseling ministry would be. It's recorded in Luke 4:18, and He said, "The Spirit of the Lord is upon me, because he hath anointed me to preach the gospel to the poor; he hath sent me to heal the broken-hearted, to preach deliverance to the captives, and recovering of sight to the blind, to set at liberty them that are bruised . . ." Jesus was saying here that He came to minister to the whole man: emotionally, mentally, financially, physically and spiritually. Most Christians aren't aware that Jesus wants to set each of us free from anything that would keep us from complete peace with Him, with our fellowman, and with ourselves. But this is why He came, and this is what He's anxious to do for you and your husband.

It's our prayer that as you spend much time in prayer and in reading God's Word, that you'll be made aware of the very presence of Jesus Christ in your life. That you'll commit your ways to Him, and then, as He makes Himself very real to you, that you'll be able to minister the healing of Jesus to your husband. There's tremendous healing power in the Word of God, Marsha, and if possible, we strongly urge you to read it aloud to your husband. The Bible says we are *washed clean and purified and healed by the reading of the Word*. And, as you read, I know you'll receive wisdom and counsel from God Himself regarding your situation, how to cope with it yourself, and how to understand and minister to your husband.

You know, David the Psalmist experienced a lot of grief and heartache during his lifetime, and in his most depressed times the Bible says he meditated on the Word of God. The result of his meditation is the beautiful book of Psalms in the Old Testament. I'm sure both of you can identify with David's innermost feelings of despair and loneliness and can say with him, "I love the Lord, because he has heard my voice and my supplications. Because he has inclined his ear to me, therefore will I call upon him as long as I live. The sorrows of death compassed me, and the pains of hell got hold upon me: I found trouble and sorrow. Then called I upon the name of the Lord; O Lord, I beseech you, deliver my soul. Gracious is the Lord, and righteous, yes, our God is merciful"! This will be your prayer and your song as you look to Him in this time of need. Let the Psalms become your personalized prayers of grief and thanksgiving before God, and experience with David the great joy of having communion with God the Father.

We don't always understand why calamity comes to us, but we do know that our greatest tragedy can be turned into God's greatest opportunity. We know that we can literally lay every problem at the feet of Jesus and watch Him perform the miracles we need. We know we can sense His closeness and presence in our lives as we praise Him and thank Him in anticipation of the way He is going to work everything out according to our good and His glory (Romans 8:28).

God always keeps His promise!

I'm sending a favorite book of mine along for you to read. Chaplain Merlin Caruthers teaches us in *Prison to Praise* the great spiritual principle of praising God in all things. I hope you can learn from it how your sorrow can be turned to joy by simply trusting God enough to praise Him in everything.

We have a good God, and He loves you and your husband and your family. David said His mercy is from everlasting to everlasting. I'm praying that you'll have a very special assurance that He's with you right now, giving you His mercy and strength and wisdom. Trust Him, dear ones. He did it for David, He'll do it for you!

God bless you,
PAT BOONE

4. THE VALLEY OF THE SHADOW

Dear Mr. Boone:

Would you please pray for my son Bobby—he has cancer. I believe God can make him well but my own faith is weak at times and I get very scared. I would never write you except for that TV program when you said you felt God does work in this world. I believe this too, but I believe faith is the key and mine gets weak at times. Please believe me, please pray for him. Please tell me if you will.

(signed) Mary Jones

Dear Mrs. Jones:

Greetings in the name of the Lord! Your letter is already in front of me, and I rejoice that God gives the Boone family the opportunity to pray for Bobby. Not only are we beginning to pray for him, but we are alerting a real "prayer army" among our friends here in California and elsewhere. Let's all commit it to the living God and for His glory. Often we pray selfishly, and God answers many of those prayers; but when we commit something to Him and ask Him to use it for His purpose and His glory I believe He is more pleased. So pray with us that not only will He touch Bobby's body, but that He will claim and use his soul for the very glory of Jesus as He did with Lazarus.

We're just sinners saved by God's grace ourselves, Mrs. Jones, and we have no more direct pipeline to God than you and Bobby do. We certainly don't know what His will is or how exactly He will answer in this case, but I do believe that we can trust Him and that by joining together in prayer and faith, and asking for His perfect will and for His own glory that we can expect a miracle!

God bless you and Bobby, and as we pray for you we hope that you'll keep us informed. Give Bobby a hug for us.

Your kinfolk in Christ,
PAT BOONE

Dear Mr. Boone:

Please forgive me for not writing sooner, but this is hard to write about. Bobby died last week. Bobby fought so hard. He rallied and seemed to improve about a week after I wrote you, but his tired little body at last just gave up.

When I wrote you I was very upset and I didn't really tell you much about Bobby. He was a sweet, open, happy boy—serious and wise far beyond his years. People I hardly knew would comment to me, often, on what a well-mannered and intelligent boy I had. My grandmother who had much experience in children would often comment on how Bobby had spoiled me for any other children because he was so well behaved. Why do we so often appreciate so much better in hindsight? Bobby also had the "faith of a little child." None of the doubts or questions adults are plagued with. He knew the Lord's Prayer at 3 years old—and even a couple of months ago, out of the blue, said to my husband and me, "What would we ever do without God and Jesus." He was expressing his wonder at the creation of the world—everything was fascinating. My husband is a teacher and he often would explain scientific facts to Bobby about nature. Bobby never seemed to forget anything. Just two months ago Bobby was lecturing all the nurses and children on the pediatrics' station on fossils—showing some limestone examples.

When Bobby died I was numb. Do you know what his last words were? They were "Pray for me." I said the Lord's Prayer and kissed him good-bye. I could feel God in the room strongly and he stopped breathing. Little children teach us to pray! Why do adults (me, I suppose) get bitter at things as we grow older? Bobby could forgive quite easily, even the pathologist that did a bone marrow puncture on his hip was forgiven. The doctor said, "I'm sorry I had to hurt you, Bobby," and Bobby said, "That's all right—you didn't hurt me, the needle did." This was last April when it all started. The memories of it all come now out of sequence.

I wonder if I can forgive like that? I've felt bitter and abandoned sometimes through all this. Relative and friends we normally expect support from, absented themselves; or if they gave help, gave it grudgingly so that I would feel guilty about being a burden. But strangers from all over have given me more kindness than I could ever dream of. Why are people like that?

I wish my faith were perfect. I wish I could know nothing would ever hurt my little one again. I believe, and yet the state of trusting, perfecting and knowing is not complete. Bobby was my firstborn—does that make a difference? So many questions run through my head. Does a child like Bobby come into the world for a short time only—for some purpose? If so—what purpose? If to suffer and die was his purpose then what is the value in any of us surviving? Doesn't growing up have a value? Bobby glorified God—that is certain—but doesn't the world need adults, too, who glorify God? Why Bobby?—who loved, enjoyed and forgave—Why him? Why the senselessness of his death? Like some beautiful little diamond—making you warm just to look at it—vanishing before your eyes. Not quickly but over five months of misery—misery of the pain of his disease and the sense of impending loss.

Was this a punishment for me? Did some evil power know just how to hurt me the most? I felt like some insect stuck on a pin, wriggling and screaming.

The physical medical facts help a little. The enemy outlined is not quite as frightening as the unknown. Bobby had lymphosarcoma, cancer of the lymphocyte or one of the white blood cells. Lymphosarcoma, leukemia and Hodgkin's disease are all in the same family called lymphoma. Lymphomas are the greatest cause of deaths of children except for accidents. And the rate of infection of lymphomas is rising. Do you remember the polio days? Every sore throat and stiff neck in children would grow gray hair for their mothers. Now we have lymphomas.

Mr. Boone—why do we spend money on bombs or space walks and all the other chrome for our national glorification when such sad things are happening to our children?

I talked to a Dr. Robert Good at the University today. Do you know what he said? "If men put all their energies toward curing pestilence, disease, starvation, and all the other human ills this would be a very nice world." He also said, "I've got a lot of brilliant scientists working on some very important projects that they can't get enough funds for and yet we are perhaps the best funded research there is." Dr. Good is perhaps the leader in pediatric cancers in the country. I wish I had a million dollars. I would give it to him. I want vengeance on that disease—I want to pound it into the ground and jump on it and say, "There! Satan! You have one less weapon against my little ones."

Please pray for Dr. Good. Men like him glorify God even if not in a formal religious way. He works so hard for the sake of little children and was so kind in talking to me today. He said he was going to Washington soon to ask for funds. Maybe your people could write their Congressmen or Senators, and even if Dr. Good doesn't get his funds, at least our politicians would know that some of us value curing disease above weapons.

Please excuse this long rambling letter. You are the first I have written since Bobby died and I'm still so uptight. I'm very grateful to you for your support you have given me. I will pray for God to bless you and your family of good Samaritans, and I ask you to include me in your prayer army.

Grace to you and Peace from God our Father and our Lord and Saviour, Jesus Christ.

Mary Jones

Dear Mary:

I hope it's all right for me to call you Mary rather than Mrs. Jones. I appreciate so much your letter and the tenderness and openness of your spirit in what has surely been a time of sorrow and testing almost greater than you can bear. Of one thing I am absolutely certain; God is not defeated in this situation, and if your faith doesn't fail, you and Bobby will be singing the praises of God together throughout all eternity. And that's a long, long time, isn't it?

I believe God directed my attention to a little sentence in a big and wonderful book the very day your letter came. I was reading in a book called *Shadow of the Almighty* by Elizabeth Elliot. She is the widow of Jim Elliot who was one of a little team of missionaries who went to Ecuador to take Christ to the Auca Indians. These Indians were head-hunting cannibals and after initially accepting him and the other missionaries into their midst, they senselessly slaughtered them! Eventually, Elizabeth Elliot and the other wives went through a training period and went back to the Aucas and now Christ has changed multitudes of the very ones who killed her husband! It's a moving story. The best part is that it's true!

I haven't read all of the book yet, but this particular morning I opened the book somewhere toward the middle, and my eye caught this statement, "I must not think it strange if God takes in youth those whom I would have kept on earth till they were older. God is peopling eternity, and I must not restrict Him to old men and women." This was a quote from Jim Elliot, and shortly after I had read that I opened your letter. Doesn't it comfort you to know that little Bobby may always be a happy child in heaven and that God had shaped his spirit and prepared him for this kind of eternal existence? Isn't it wonderful to think that God desires the presence of little children and young boys and girls around Him in heaven as well as the company of adults and older people?

We are only able to see things from the human viewpoint; it's very hard for us to get any kind of a glimpse into what eternity will be like. Even Solomon said that his long and full and varied life (more so than anyone who ever lived) was all vanity and like a vapor that disappears quickly and signifies nothing. This life, no matter what happens to us, while we have mortal bodies, must be like the briefest of birth pains ushering us into the fuller and richer and perfect existence that God has prepared for those who love Him. As you know, Bobby loves Him, and is now in the bosom of his Creator.

Jim Elliot was 20 years old when he prayed, "Lord, make my way prosperous, not that I achieve high station, but that my life may be an exhibit to the value of knowing God." His prayer has been richly answered, even though his mortal life ended. His witness for Christ and the glory of God continues on and on. I feel sure, Mary, that Bobby's story and witness has not come to an end. It's not for us to strive and try to decide just how God will use his life and his story, but if we just leave it to Him and believe Him, little Bobby's life will bring glory to Jesus. What more could any of us want, when it's all said and done?

Our prayers now are for you and Bobby's close relatives. Bobby's battle is won and he's already achieved the goal that all of us seek—the literal presence of God! So now we all need to be praying that God will help us to achieve the same victory. I agree with you about the insanity of spending millions to go to the moon while millions of human beings suffer under ailments that God would help us conquer if we would simply turn our abilities and our earning power and our intelligence over to Him. But man is this way; and the devil is the prince of this world. I'm afraid there are only individual answers to individual problems, and that's the business God is in. Nations and civilizations go down to destruction, but God saves the faithful individuals whose trust is in Him. That's you and me—and Bobby. Praise the living God!

Your brother in Jesus,
PAT BOONE

PART FOUR: ON THE LIGHTER SIDE

1. Overcoming Fear
2. The Mouse and I
3. Why I Became a Jew
4. God on the Night Shift

1. OVERCOMING FEAR

Dear Mr. Boone:

I live in the east where . thunder storms are very prevalent. My summers are one long battle with dread and anxiety because I have a very real fear of lightning. . . .

Dear Pat Boone:

I am deeply concerned about my wife. I have a very good job which I like but it forces me to travel a good deal which means being often away from home. Although we live in a quiet suburb with good near neighbors, my wife grows more and more afraid to be left alone with the children. . . .

Dear Pat:

I've been a Boy Scout ever since I was old enough to join a Cub Pack. Now I'm an Explorer Scout and our leader takes us into the High Sierras. I hate to admit it, and I don't know if you can understand, but when we are in very high places like at the top of a steep cliff I get sick with fear. . . .

This is only a sampling of the letters I get about *fear*. So this answer is addressed to *YOU*, if you are afraid.

So many of us are facing fears and uncertainty on every hand; this is an age of depression and anxiety, psychiatrists are flourishing as never before, trying to help people cope with their phobias, their tensions, their anxieties and private terrors. Every night on television there is another prophet of doom, and more predictions of coming disaster. Is it any wonder that people are afraid? People today need miracles!

That goes for me and my family, too. And because we've experienced so many miracles in the last several years, I've written a new book for Revell called *A Miracle a Day Keeps the Devil Away*. It's a collection of 31 separate miraculous happenings that have involved me and my family and close friends. These miracles have virtually banished fear from our lives, and we want to share them with you. The Bible says that "God is no respecter of persons," and what He's done for us, He waits to do for you.

This miracle, recorded in the book, concerns my own wife, Shirley, and one of her deepest fears, the fear of flying. Psychiatrists can't do much about that fear, and if God can solve that one—He can handle *any* fear or phobia! As you read Shirley's story, you might just substitute your own personal fear for hers: the prescription is the same.

How are you at flying?

I don't mean to dig up that terrible old joke, "I just flew in from Chicago and, boy, are my arms tired!"

I mean if and when you fly in an airplane, can you relax and enjoy it? Do you just sit back and revel in the luxury, the miracle of modern air travel, eating the food that's brought, reading a magazine, and gazing with awe and delight at the passing landscapes thirty thousand feet below?

Or are you a "white-knuckle" flyer?

Are there giant butterflies already airborne in your stomach three days before *you* take off? Is there a feeling of controlled panic in your breast as the stewardess closes the EXIT door? Do you have to tranquilize yourself with pills or booze before, during, and after the flight? Do you secretly grip the seat till your hands turn white, and then green? Is there a deep feeling of dread that you'll never see your loved ones again; does a vivid picture keep flashing through your mind of the plane you're in hurtling toward the ground—till you wish you'd never planned the trip?

At every bump or air pocket, do you wish you'd

increased your insurance? While you're in the air, do you learn what it is to "pray without ceasing"?

Then this miracle is for you.

My wife, Shirley, was in that second category all her life, until Jesus changed her. She was a real white-knuckle flyer, nervous and apprehensive for days before flight time, constantly looking for reasons she shouldn't go at all. She'd *never* fly alone, and yet was frightened for us to travel together, picturing our daughters with nobody to bring them up. The only solution was not to fly at all—and that's what she did, whenever it was possible.

Lots of entertainers are like that; some of the biggest stars of all have *never* flown! And many, many of the rest go by train or boat whenever possible, even passing up terrific career opportunities if flying is involved. Other entertainers, athletes and business people who absolutely *have* to fly spend thousands on psychiatrists, hypnotists and gurus (pharmacists and distillers), so that they can handle the uncontrollable fear that wells up in them at the thought of leaving the ground.

Stewardesses report that their biggest problem is handling folks who get absolutely potted in the air. Yet they know that it's *fear* that causes the passengers to drink and without the alcoholic "pain-killer" most of them couldn't (or wouldn't) dare to fly. Sad, but true.

Well, Shirley never drank to escape her fear—she just lived with it! And so did the rest of us, because fear and anxieties have an infectious quality that communicates to others, breeding irritability and short tempers and even physical discomforts.

But in her best-selling book, *One Woman's Liberation*,[2] she describes the turning point in her spiritual life, her encounter with Jesus as Baptizer in the Holy Spirit. In intimate detail, she shares the disintegration of our life together and her own rising insecurity and loss of identity

[2]Shirley Boone, *One Woman's Liberation.* Creation House Inc., Carol Stream, Ill., 1972.

that brought about an inner vacuum which led her to prayer and the Bible—and to Jesus.

Tortured by feelings of inadequacy and failure, and fearing she'd even lost her capacity to love, she dropped to her knees in our bedroom, alone, and asked the Lord to take over her life completely, to cleanse her of all her soul-stains, and to fill her with Himself, to baptize her in His own Holy Spirit.

And He did—right then!

Though you really can't describe such a moment adequately, she says that when she'd said everything she could think of in English, expressing her deep need and her hunger for the touch of Jesus, *she continued to offer Him the sound of her voice*, praying that the Lord would accept her poor offering and fashion it into a miracle of praise, according to the promise and example of passages like John 1:33; Mark 16:17; Acts 2:4; 10:44-47; Romans 8:27; and 1 Corinthians 14:2.

Shirley realized that *45 minutes* had been consumed with praise and adoration! She couldn't even have imagined such a thing before, and it left such an "afterglow" of peace and wellbeing.

Now, friend, as wonderful (or impossible) as this sounds, it didn't stop there.

I hadn't *had* this Baptism in the Holy Spirit experience, and neither had anybody else in my whole family; it would be at least six months before I came to my own encounter with Jesus as Baptizer. And though Shirley told me all about it, I had so many questions and doctrinal reservations and personal inhibitions that I might never have asked the Lord to fill me in the same way: *if I hadn't seen my wife change before my eyes into a different kind of woman!*

The Shirley I'd come to know—a volatile, changeable, up-and-down emotional chameleon; an increasingly troubled, anxious, insecure, nervous, and physical wreck—was transformed day by day into a stable, confident, secure, warm, and loving person; healthy and giving and quietly ready for any of life's crises! It was amazing. It was impossible. It was a *miracle!*

Humanly speaking, two very dramatic evidences proved that something supernatural had happened. First, I saw love in Shirley's eyes for me. Love I had forfeited and lost, and had no real expectation of ever seeing again. Lost love is almost impossible to regain, and yet Shirley was drawing on some invisible source, and seeing qualities in me I didn't know were there.

And second, I discovered *she'd lost her fear of flying!*

I say *I* discovered it, because she didn't seem to realize it! I was watching her very closely during the six months after her Baptism, and we flew a number of times in that period. There was no *fear*, no apprehension, no display of nerves, or even tension before, during, or after a flight—no "white knuckles," no suppressed panic. It just didn't seem to *matter* to Shirley anymore whether she was on the ground or in the air!

I finally mentioned it to her one day after we took off and the pilot had turned off the seat belt signs. Her eyes widened, she thought a second, and said, "You're right! I hadn't even thought about it. I'm not afraid anymore—not at all! Praise the Lord!"

And that was that. Even when she consciously thought about the possibility of a crash, tried to picture the plane going down, even when we'd hit an air pocket or real rough weather, she said she felt like she was literally cradled in the hands of God, and unless He permitted it, *nothing* could force that plane off its course. So what was there to worry about!

That's a miracle.

You ask a psychiatrist if he can literally *take away a person's fear;* he hopes to help the person live with it, adjust to it, control it. Ask a so-called positive thinker the same question; he'll try to help a person concentrate on something else, persuade himself he's *not* afraid. Ask a hypnotist; he'll try to get the person's subconscious to take over, and hide the fear from his *consciousness. None* of them can just take the fear away—for good.

Only God can do that.

Through Paul, the Lord advises, "And be not conformed to this world, but be ye transformed by the renewing of your mind . . ." (Romans 12:2).

But how in the world can a person have his or her mind *renewed?* You can have a tire recapped, a sofa recovered, a physical organ replaced, maybe. But a mind renewed? How?

Paul explained it to Timothy: *"For God hath not given us the spirit of fear; but of power, and of love, and of a sound mind"* (2 Timothy 1:7). He wrote to Titus: "Not by works of righteousness which we have done, but according to his mercy he saved us, by the washing of regeneration, and *renewing of the Holy Spirit;* which He shed on us abundantly through Jesus Christ our Saviour" (see Titus 3:5-6).

Shirley experienced the absolute reality of this spiritual operation, as well as these words from the apostle John: "There is no fear in love, but *perfect love casteth out fear:* because fear hath torment. He that feareth is not made perfect in love" (see 1 John 4:18).

And how do you come by this perfect love that casts out fear? Paul again: ". . . the love of God is shed abroad in our hearts *by the Holy Spirit which is given unto us"* (see Romans 5:5).

Shirley says that if she got on a plane and walked back to her seat—and found Jesus of Nazareth sitting in the seat next to hers, she'd feel pretty relaxed about the flight! How could you worry, sitting next to the Master of earth and sky, the One who stilled the wind and sea with a word? Wouldn't His presence make *you* feel pretty secure?

Well, we both know that Jesus has His reservation on any flight we make, because He said, "Lo, I am with you always, even unto the end of the world" (Matthew 28:20). Oh, if we'd only believe Him!

And why *don't* we believe Him? Paul hit it again; "But I fear, lest by any means, *as the serpent beguiled Eve through his craftiness, so your minds should be corrupted* from the simplicity that is in Christ" (see 2 Corinthians 11:3).

See why we need miracles? Because we're in a supernatural struggle with a mightily endowed supernatural enemy, who intends to rob and destroy us! We can't even *see* him as Eve could, to defend ourselves!

There's only One who can see the devil, and knows his plans—and He offers us supernatural assistance, with a 100 percent guarantee of victory! Shirley, in her simple, trusting way, obeyed Jesus' words: "Seek ye first the kingdom of God, and his righteousness: and everything you need will be given to you" (see Matthew 6:33); and His assurance, "The Father knows what you need *before you ask*" (see Matthew 6:8), became real! She couldn't know the next few years would require thousands of miracles for her. But the Father did, and as she sought Him first, His love filled her and simply left no room for fear![3]

But we're making our reservations for *another* flight, another miracle in the air:

"For the Lord himself shall descend from heaven with a shout, with the voice of the archangel, and with the trump of God: and the dead in Christ shall rise first: Then we which are alive and remain shall be caught up together with them *in the clouds, to meet the Lord in the air:* and so shall we ever be with the Lord. Wherefore, comfort one another with these words" (1 Thessalonians 4:16-18).

[3]Pat Boone, *A Miracle a Day Keeps the Devil Away.* Fleming H. Revell, Old Tappan, N.J., 1974.

2. THE MOUSE AND I

Dear Pat Boone:

I know that you are the father of teenagers, as am I. I have two teenage daughters and a son. Their mother was a shining Christian woman, although I guess I was what you might call lukewarm—the Christmas-Easter-always-send-the-children-to-Sunday-School variety who trusted in my wife's prayers to do the job for the family. Since we lost her a few years ago I've tried very hard to grow as a Christian and to help them continue in the way she would want them to go. We pray together sometimes; but if I am honest I must admit that I have reservations. When they want to confide all their problems and needs, large and small, to God in prayer I am almost apprehensive and discourage it. What will happen to their faith if He doesn't answer? It's almost as if they expect miracles and that worries me. Have you had to handle this situation?

Thanks in advance for any help you can give me,
George Snow

Dear George:

Indeed I have "had to handle this situation" and I know the pangs you feel. I suspect almost every Christian parent does. Perhaps this is why a particular "happening" in our own family which I recounted in my book *A Miracle a Day Keeps the Devil Away*[3] was particularly meaningful to me—and may be to you. It has to do with a father, a daughter, a mouse, and the Creator of all three.

[3]Pat Boone, *A Miracle a Day Keeps the Devil Away*. Fleming H. Revell, Old Tappan, N.J., 1974.

"Daddy, please—can you take me to the vet right away?"

My second daughter, Lindy, then 14, who reminds me so much of an Indian princess in her dark beauty, stood before me, giant tears filling her eyes. In her cupped hands she held a little brown mouse, curled up and still, apparently lifeless. It had been a Christmas present from her best friend, and was precious to her already.

I looked at the wee creature, saw just the faintest trace of breathing, and experienced that familiar sinking feeling a parent knows when a child asks so earnestly for something that's probably impossible. And—I looked up again into those big, brown, brimming-over eyes of Lindy's, anxious and hoping and imploring, and knew I had to try.

But what?

"I'll call the guy at the pet store and see what he says." Lindy followed me to the phone in the pantry, still holding the mouse in the cup of her hands.

The man at the store laughed when I told him the problem. "I'm sorry," he said, "but it is sort of funny. There's nothing anybody can do. Just throw it in the trash and come on down. We'll give you another one. A sick mouse is a dead mouse."

Throw it in the trash? He obviously couldn't see the look on Lindy's face. I thanked him and phoned the vet, Dr. Miller.

Again, I could sense the amusement on the other end of the line. "Oh, no, Mr. Boone, there's no point in bringing the mouse over here. I couldn't help you. You should probably just replace it."

I thanked him for his time and hung the phone up, feelings clashing inside me. Part of me wanted to stage a grand burial (we'd done that before with Debby's iguana) and then go pick out a new mouse, maybe two. But another part of me was reaching desperately to God, asking Him for a miracle *now!*

"Come on, Lindy, let's go upstairs."

She knew I meant we were going to the bedroom to pray. Little Laury, our youngest, had joined us, having instant empathy for Lindy and the mouse, and wanting to help in any way she could.

On the way up the stairs, I thought, *"What* am I *doing?* That little mouse is almost dead. Why should I risk Lindy's faith this way? Is God really concerned about such a trivial thing? And what will it do to my daughters if He doesn't do something?"

Still, it seemed the only chance we had, and in a moment we had closed the bedroom door and were kneeling around the bed, crying out to the Lord.

"Father, didn't Jesus teach us to bring our every concern to You? Didn't He say that You take notice of every bird and flower, and number the very hairs on our heads? And didn't He actually say that if we had enough faith we could speak to a mountain and see it moved into the sea?

"Well, Lord, we believe Your Word.

"And right now, we're not concerned with a mountain. It's this little mouse. Nobody can help it but You, Lord. The pet store man can't, and the vet can't, and we can't. Only You, Lord. And You made this little animal—You must love it more than we do. Please, heal this little thing, give it life."

Something I'd been reading just that morning in John's Gospel flashed before me. "Jesus, remember when You called Lazarus from the tomb? Just before You commanded the dead man into life, You *thanked God out loud* in front of everybody, because You knew He was hearing You! Well, Lord, we know You hear us, and so we want to thank You right now."

And we did. For a couple of minutes, it seemed so right to just thank the Lord and express our love to Him. Our hands went up in the air, as if bearing a literal gift to our Father, and tears of real joy ran down our cheeks. It was not till later that I learned Lindy had felt the mouse twitch *just as we began to thank the Lord,* and she had tearfully placed him on the bed without opening her eyes. Not knowing if it was living or dead, she gave herself to praise, thanking God for His goodness.

And somehow, together, we *knew!*

We opened our eyes and right before us on the corner of the bed, that little mouse was sitting up, weakly rubbing its face with its front paws!

It seemed awfully shaky, but while we watched, laughing and crying and praising God all at the same time, it appeared to gain strength every minute! Lindy ran and brought back some seeds and lettuce, but though it made a feeble attempt to crack a seed, the little mouse seemed still too weak and just nibbled a little lettuce and drank some water that Laury had brought.

In a couple of minutes, though, it rummaged around for a seed it had shoved under itself for future reference and cracked it and began to eat! That was all we needed to see. We knew it was just a matter of time—that the patient was on the road to recovery. And sure enough, in just a little while, the Miracle Mouse (that's what we named it) was running around like crazy, more full of life than ever!

But wait—that's not all.

Lindy began to cry again, even while we knelt by the bed, watching the mouse regain its strength. "What's the matter, honey?" I asked her.

"Daddy," she answered, when she could sort of get herself together. "I just realized that God has answered another prayer, probably more important than our prayer for the mouse.

"A few days ago, some of my friends and I got into a big discussion about God, and this boy, a couple of years older than the rest of us—and very smart—laughed at us and showed us in some pretty logical-sounding ways that there couldn't be a God. I really didn't believe him, but I didn't have answers that could change his mind, and I did sort of feel foolish.

"I stopped praying for a couple of days, and really have been feeling sort of confused and lousy and irritable, and separated from God and you all, too."

The tears started rolling again, but she continued, "Just yesterday I prayed, 'God, if You're there, and hear me, please show me that You're real. And dear God, show me in some way that's not logical!'

"Daddy, I know that's why this happened. God *does* hear me and He *does* answer our prayers, and we just can't *ever* understand that with our logic, can we?

"Thank you, Daddy."

Well . . . my hands went up again, and looking heavenward through my own flowing tears I cried, "Thank You, Father." (See Romans 8:15.)

Things were different in our house after that. We were much more bold about coming to God in faith, trusting Him with anything and everything. And eventually, reading again the story of Lazarus, I saw that the reason for His miracle and ours was the same. "That you might see the glory of God" (see John 11:40).

Yours in the Fatherhood of God,
PAT BOONE

3. WHY I BECAME A JEW

Dear Pat Boone:

More and more I hear you talking about Jewish things on television. I know you have done TV spots with your daughter, Cherry, encouraging people to give to the United Jewish Appeal. I've also heard you say proudly that your daughter has learned to read and write Hebrew, and I have seen your television special that you did with your family, "The Pat Boone Family in the Holy Land." I also know that you wrote the words for "Exodus"—my question is, have you converted to Judaism?

Yours sincerely,
Hobart Aske

Dear Mr. Aske:

Yes, I have!

My whole family and I have become Jewish, although only by adoption. Obviously, we can't go back and be born into a racially Jewish family. But we have fallen in love with all that is truly Jewish, and my oldest daughter will be married in a Hebrew-Christian ceremony. She's marrying Dan O'Neill who, like her, reads and writes Hebrew, and has spent 13 months on two kibbutzim in Israel—and was living and working on a kibbutz during the Yom Kippur war. For several years now, we have had Hanukkah parties in our home, and have hosted a number of gatherings of Jewish people, religious and otherwise.

Why?

Aren't we Christians? Yes, we are. But so was Sammy

Davis, at least by heritage. So was Elizabeth Taylor. So were lots of other people, entertainers and folks in other walks of life, when they "became Jews"; that is, they studied the Hebrew writings and traditions, and were "adopted into" the family of "God's chosen people." I think I understand very well why they made this choice, and the spiritual search that led them to that crossroads in their lives.

They were dissatisfied with the half-measures they had encountered in organized religion. They had been turned off by the "shadow games" that so often take place in church buildings and religious groups. They were looking for reality, for roots, for heritage; and somehow, continuity and *contact with God.*

We all need that, and most religions promise it—but few people ever experience contact with God, regardless of their religion. That's the trouble with most religions: they act like *inoculations.* They give you a mild "dose," and make you immune to the real thing. That's why I've said for quite some time that the last thing the world needs today is more religion; what we need is *relationship.* Relationship with God, and relationship with each other.

And I'm sure it's the need, the thirst, for that kind of relationship that drew Elizabeth Taylor and Sammy Davis and me to a deep consideration of Judaism.

Believe me, when you read that Old Testament and you take a look at Abraham and Moses and Joshua and Elijah and Gideon and David, you can see people who had living, breathing *relationships* with the God of all creation. And that's exciting! I guess we'd all like to have that kind of experience with the One who put all this together, and who would talk to us and deal with us on a one-to-one basis, wouldn't we?

Judaism, historically, has seemed to offer that.

I used to chafe a little bit (and millions of people still do) at the idea that the Jews were God's "chosen people." Why should *they* be chosen? What was so special about them? Oh, I knew there was supposed to be some vague connection between the Jews of the Old Testament and Jesus and modern day Christianity, but the thread of connection seemed almost invisible to me. I believed the Bible, and therefore felt that Adam and Abraham and Moses and David were *my* spiritual ancestors, somehow, but I wasn't *Jewish*, and I felt just as "chosen" as anybody else!

What does "God's chosen people" mean, anyway?

Several years ago I found out, as I read through the Old Testament Scriptures. I was startled first to find that *Abraham wasn't Jewish!* Although God promised Abraham (Genesis 12) that "in thee shall all families of the earth be blessed" and "I will make of thee a great nation" and "I will bless them that bless thee, and curse him that curseth thee," the people of Israel did not begin until *Jacob* wrestled with God (Genesis 35) and insisted upon a blessing from God, and received this promise: "Israel shall be thy name; and *he called his name Israel.* And God said unto him, I am God Almighty: be fruitful and multiply; a nation and a company of nations shall be of thee, and kings shall come out of thy loins; and the land which I gave Abraham and Isaac, to thee I will give it, and to thy seed after thee will I give the land."

The people of Israel, the Jews, began officially with Israel himself, or Jacob. Abraham is called "the father of the faithful," and God's blessing and promise came to him because "he believed in the Lord; and he counted it to him for righteousness" (Genesis 15:6). Today, Moslems and Christians *and* Jews revere Abraham as their spiritual ancestor and human example of faith in God. But it was not until Moses, long after Abraham, Isaac and Jacob, that God spoke these words: "For thou art an holy people unto the Lord thy God: the Lord thy God *hath chosen thee to be a special people unto himself,* above all people that are upon the face of the earth" (Deuteronomy 7:6).

And those words sound fine, if God's message ended there. But it doesn't. He goes on through the seventh and eighth chapters of Deuteronomy to outline what it means to be "chosen" by God. God expects those that He chooses in some special way to keep His commandments, and *to be examples* of personal relationship with Him—or suffer dire consequences. In fact, He warns in Deuteronomy 8:20 that if these people, the Jews, did not keep His commandments and walk faithfully before Him that "as the nations which the Lord destroyeth before your face, so shall *ye* perish; because ye would not be obedient unto the voice of the Lord your God."

Suddenly, the idea of being "God's chosen people" might start to lose some of its appeal.

I've seen in my study that God deliberately chose these fiery, stubborn, softhearted but hardheaded people to be *"an example,"* an example of what it meant to come into covenant relationship with the Living God, to be blessed at His hand, but also to be punished for disobedience. I saw that God didn't *love* the Jew more than He does the Arab or the Syrian or the Chinese. He simply made a choice, because of His promise to Abraham and to Isaac and Jacob, to use the Jew as "Exhibit A" of the way He wants to deal with all human beings.

Throughout the Old Testament history, I saw that whenever the Jew loved and praised and obeyed God, he was blessed above all people. Whenever he wandered away and forgot God, and abandoned His instruction, he began to be cursed and afflicted and oppressed. Therefore, to be "chosen" by God is to become eligible for great blessings—and fearful persecution.

The trouble was, it was impossible to *keep* all of God's commandments. Human nature being what it is, it seemed more and more hopeless for man to please God by his obedience.

Finally, through the prophet Amos, God warned: "You only have I known of all the families of the earth: therefore I will punish you for all your iniquities. Can two walk together, except they be agreed?" (Amos 3:2-3).

The Jew found it impossible to keep step with God, on His terms. Finally, in Amos 9:9-10, God said, "For lo, I will command, and *I will sift the house of Israel among all nations,* like as corn is sifted in a sieve, yet shall not the least grain fall upon the earth. All the sinners of my people shall die by the sword, which say, The evil shall not overtake nor prevent us."

And it happened just as God said it would. These "chosen people" were scattered all over the world, and have just begun to be drawn back together, according to the promise He made in the last verse of that book, "And I will plant them (again) upon their land, and they shall no more be pulled up out of their land which I have given them, saith the Lord thy God."

Actually, the history of "God's chosen people" has been so anguished these last several thousand years, you might wonder why anybody would want to be identified with them. And few would, I suppose, except that God promised *a Messiah* through the seed (or offspring) of David. He promised that He would *bless all the nations of the world,* as He had told Abraham, through a divine God-Man who would bear the guilt and sin of the world's disobedience Himself, and restore man to God, in a one-to-one relationship.

And God deliberately and lovingly *chose* that this Messiah should come through the Jew!

He promised in Micah 5:2 that this Messiah would be born in Bethlehem; in Isaiah 7:14 that He would be born of a virgin; in Deuteronomy 18 that He would be "a prophet" like Moses; in Isaiah 53:9,6 that He would live a sinless life and be offered as a sacrificial lamb as the final atonement for sin; in Psalm 22 that He would die by crucifixion; in Isaiah 53 that He would be the final sacrifice for sin; and in Psalm 16 that He would arise from the dead!

All these things God promised the Jew.

The matchless prophet Isaiah, looking down through the centuries at this promised Messiah, said,

"He is despised and rejected of men, a man of sorrows,

and acquainted with grief: and we hid as it were our faces from him; he was despised, and we esteemed him not. Surely He hath borne *our griefs*, and carried our sorrows: yet we did esteem him stricken, smitten of God, and afflicted.

"But he was wounded for our transgressions, he was bruised for our iniquities; the chastisement of *our* peace was upon him; and with his stripes *we* are healed" (Isaiah 53:3–5).

To me, all these passages of Scripture point toward the rabbi from Nazareth, the man Jesus, who stood up in the synagogue at the beginning of His ministry, opened the book of Isaiah and read some of the Messianic prophecies—then closed the book, "and gave it again to the minister, and sat down. And the eyes of all them that were in the synagogue were fastened on him, and he began to say unto them, *This day is this Scripture fulfilled in your ears*" (Luke 4).

As I read through the New Testament account, I saw this peasant Jew travel through Israel for three years, performing miracles every day and fulfilling all the Messianic prophecies leading up to the crucifixion and the resurrection. I heard Him say, "I did not come to destroy the law and the prophets, *but to fulfill them.*" (See Matthew 5:17.) What a stupendous, incredible and humanly impossible statement to make. Either this man, Yeshua, was a demented egomaniac, or He was what He claimed to be! There are only those two possibilities.

When my family and I were in Israel a couple of years ago, we discovered that Jews everywhere in that land acknowledge that there was a historical Yeshua who lived around the Sea of Galilee, who performed wonderful miracles, who was crucified outside the city of Jerusalem, and who was "a wonderful teacher." Their faith in the reality of the man Jesus was stronger in most cases than many Christians in *this* country. But how could a man be a "wonderful teacher" and a demented egomaniac at the same time?

He was either the Messiah, as He claimed—or He wasn't.

And if He *was*, then He was the fulfillment of God's promise to Abraham, to Isaac and Jacob, to Moses and the children of Israel, to Isaiah and Amos and every faithful Jew who ever lived. And He made it possible for me, a Gentile, to get *in* on it! He made it possible for every human being to have that kind of one-to-one relationship with God that Gideon and Joshua and Moses had!

Yeshua, Jesus, makes it possible for me to become a Jew: by adoption! The Jewish fisherman, John, wrote, "He came unto his own and his own received him not. But as many as received him, *to them gave he power to become the sons of God*, even to them that believe on his name" (John 1:11-12).

And the eminent Jewish scholar, Saul of Tarsus (or Paul), wrote: "For the wages of sin is death; but the gift of God is eternal life through Messiah Yeshua our Lord" (see Romans 6:23). Paul, in that letter to the Romans—or Gentiles—also spent a lot of time in the tenth and eleventh chapters explaining to the Gentiles that they were very fortunate to have become "adopted Jews" through the sacrifice of Yeshua.

This has been a very long answer to your question, but it takes a long time, and a lot of words, to try to undo the insidious distortion that history has worked on the claims of Jesus. What started out in the first century as a "Jewish" religion as the fulfillment of all the Messianic prophecies—which Gentiles could gratefully become part of—eventually became thought of as a "Gentile" religion and has often actually taken on anti-Semitic qualities, and apparently been alien to the Jews who gave it birth.

Yes, I have become a Jew. My whole family have become Jews, following the Rabbi and Messiah Yeshua. We have placed our lives and destinies in the hands of the Carpenter from Nazareth who gave His life for us and about whom John proclaimed: "Behold, the Lamb of God, who taketh away the sins of the world!"

Yours in the brotherhood of Moses and Yeshua,
PAT BOONE

4. GOD ON THE NIGHT SHIFT

Dear Reader:

Do you believe that Bible promises are kept?

I not only believe they are but it has been proven over and over in my life. Take this one: "Cast thy bread upon the waters: for thou shalt find it after many days" (Ecclesiastes 11:1). That is the promise. Pondering on that I came to believe that, through writing books or answering letters asking for help, I am trying in whatever way I can out of my own experience or insight to "cast my bread upon the waters."

When I sent a copy of *A Miracle a Day* to a dear Catholic Sister it was because I knew Sister Joseph Bernard works with people all the time, people with all kinds of problems, and hoped this book might be some kind of inspiration or help to *her.* But truly there is no such thing as a one-way flow in the fellowship of Christ. For after not too many days Sister sent back a letter that has been such an inspiration and help to *me* that I'd like to share it with you.

Yours in the joy of Christ,
PAT BOONE

Dear Pat:

Your autographed book arrived the day before I left for the West. Then on my return I had the flu. Hence, the delay in acknowledging the receipt of the book.

Though I belong to a different organization, we certainly worship the same God who daily performs His miracles. If people can pause for a moment after an unusual incident, they would not call the incidents coincidence, but rather real miracles. I recognized the workings of God in our daily lives early in my nursing career. Let me give you an illustration.

As a night supervisor of a 300-bed hospital, I used to make the rounds of the very ill patients *every* night before I visited the other patients. On leaving the room, I usually touched their hands or head and said, "Have a good night." On one occasion, when I returned the following evening a badly arthritic patient said to me, "Oh, Sister, bless me again as you did last night. I slept all night for the first time." I told her that I merely touched her hand; I did not bless her. I then explained, "Mrs. Sheme, it was *your* faith in the God whom I represent that helped you."

As you know, Pat, faith can certainly move mountains—and can spread as well. For example, the patient in the bed opposite Mrs. Sheme was having a gallbladder attack and was sitting at the side of her bed with an emesis basin under her chin. She called to me and said, "Sister, I am not a Catholic, but I believe; bless me too." She was very, very miserable. So I went to the side of her bed and made a small sign of the cross on her forehead. I felt so sorry for her. Her attack subsided and she slept all night.

These daily miracles are common occurrences in our lives. I depend on them to keep "my marbles" in my daily work. After my initial attempt to try to solve a problem, I call on the Lord if I seem to get no place. The result: I don't get ulcers. What I can't solve and the Lord doesn't see fit to solve it, I accept and live with it. But what often happens is that it ceases to be a problem—but another miracle.

On another occasion, I was assisting a dying patient who was really suffering despite medication. After she died, knowing that she had faith in her suffering, I said, "Catherine, if you are in heaven, find my flashlight for me." I had misplaced it the evening before. I then left the room to make my rounds in another part of the building. As I entered the first room, I was greeted with, "Sister, here is your flashlight. You left it here last night." I had no reason for going into that room first. You can imagine my reaction. I looked heavenward and quietly said, "Thank you, Saint Catherine."

I want you to know, Pat, that your book will reach more people than you will ever know. As long as the message gets across, you will be happy.

Thank you ever so much for sharing your daily miracles. It is refreshing to know that others are not ashamed to relate the occurrences. I can read and reread the book and experience the same feeling of awe the second time. May God reward you and your family for all that you are doing for Him.

Be assured of my own prayerful remembrance that God will continue to bless you, your work and family!

Sincerely and prayerfully,
Sister Joseph Bernard

PART FIVE: THE FRACTURED FAMILY

1. How Parents Help Teenagers Deal with Sex Temptations

Shirley Boone Answers: What mothers should know best about sex and Satan

Pat Boone Answers: What fathers should know best about the "new morality"

2. A Fallen Woman — Age Seventeen
3. Sex Problems in Marriage
4. Abortion

1. HOW PARENTS HELP TEENAGERS DEAL WITH SEX TEMPTATIONS

Dear Pat Boone:

My son and daughter, both in high school, have taken to discussing (favorably) the idea of "trial marriage" as advanced by the so-called "new morality." How is a Christian father to deal with far-out, farfetched approach to sex? I simply don't know how to talk to them. . . .

Dear Mrs. Boone:

My daughter's best friend has decided at 16 that the highest aspiration in life is to be a Playboy Bunny. She spends most of her time and all her allowance on beauty preparations and flirting. She isn't the only one. What can a Christian mother *do?* . . .

Dear Pat and Shirley Boone:

How can Christian parents help their teenagers deal with the rising sex temptations facing them? . . .

Sounds repetitious, doesn't it? But that's what comes in our mail day after day. What seems remarkable to me is that they come addressed to *us*—members of the entertainment community in Beverly Hills and Hollywood, certainly at one time considered synonymous with Sodom and Gomorrah. Perhaps it is because they feel that we, and our daughters, see a good deal of raw temptation here. And we do. Perhaps because word is going throughout the land about what God is doing in this entertainment community—that we are blessed by being part of it. And we are.

Exciting things *are* happening to whole families in homes all over Hollywood and Beverly Hills, including ours.

As exhibit "A", I present my own wife, Shirley, who has been through an amazing transformation. When I first knew her as a teenage, high school girl, and through the first years of our marriage, she was always a rather shy, private person who had a few very good friends, who wanted to be a good wife and mother, and that was it. Look at her now: she's singing with me on television and on stage, flying to Israel and Tokyo for family appearances, speaking on national television and around the country in person and has written a best-selling book.

Is this the same Shirley I married?

It is—with a difference! And I love the difference.

And I love the fact that she deserves top billing here in answering all those concerned mothers for she worked it out carefully, prayerfully, and wisely before she wrote *One Woman's Liberation?*[2]

Shirley Boone Answers: What mothers should know best about sex and Satan

Dear, *dear* Concerned Mothers:

In a newspaper interview a year or so ago, Los Angeles Superior Court Judge John Shilder concluded, "Many young people now barely believe in *death*, much less the devil."

In earlier times when the infant mortality rate was high and several generations lived under one roof, boys and girls were made aware of the frailty of life by deaths within their households. They saw baby brothers and sisters die, as well as great-uncles and grandmothers. Right in the next room! So it's obvious they thought about eternity and God and the devil.

[2]Shirley Boone, *One Woman's Liberation*. Creation House Inc., Carol Stream, Ill., 1972.

Now, however, most babies live, while the elderly are isolated from the young. Grandma and Grandpa are left behind in Iowa, or they're snugly settled in "retirement communities" closed to youthful residents, so that adolescents don't see their infirmities.

Today, when death does touch a family, it usually comes in a hospital, not in the back bedroom. So, to summarize Judge Shilder's thought: boys and girls have little occasion to ponder death on a personal level, much less the hereafter. And the devil, like "The Invisible Man," runs unnoticed and unchecked, creating heartbreak and havoc.

Our daughters believe in the devil because the Bible tells them he exists; Pat and I tell them he exists; and they see his works which tell them the same thing.

And, odd though this may sound to many of you, Pat and I consider the girls' knowledge of Satan part of their sex education. By this, I certainly don't mean that we think sex is sin. Far from it! *But the temptation to misuse it,* like the temptation to misuse any of God's gifts, *comes from the devil.*

When the young people accept this, they don't become instantly infallible. Recognition of the devil is no chastity belt. But it *is* easier to avoid a pitfall if you know that it's waiting for you, and who dug it for you, and why.

Therefore, while boys and girls are learning the clinical aspects of sex, they should also be reminded that God and the devil each have a use for the exciting new urges they are experiencing.

As Richard Hogue points out in his excellent book, *Sex and the Jesus Kids,* " 'The devil made me do it' is no joke. In fact, Satan himself is the enemy—he's trying everything in the world to destroy this generation with sex—and, though the pressure may come from a thousand different directions, *Satan is the problem.* And you'll never get victory until you realize that *there is a devil* who's out to get you."

Parents should forewarn their children about Satan in

the same way that they take them to their pediatrician for Salk antipolio vaccine, as an important protective measure. However, a warning about the devil isn't enough to guarantee a lifetime of immunity to transgression, anymore than a single vaccination is enough to guarantee a lifetime of immunity to polio. Therefore, supplementary procedures (or spiritual "booster shots") are necessary in the form of further parental advice and control.

It's amazing how quickly little boys and girls discover that they *are* boys and girls—and that there's a difference!

I'm sure our eldest daughter, Cherry, wasn't a day over six years old when a boy no older than she was, sent her a heart-shaped box of candy for Valentine's Day and a *ring*. He sent them all the way to England, too, because that's where we were at the time. While Cherry was still in the first grade, she talked about being engaged! Then when Lindy was about the same age, she and Terry Taylor, Robert Taylor's son, had a big crush on each other. They swapped rings and really considered themselves romantically linked for years.

Of course, in every generation, children have probably talked about their "sweethearts" but, watching our daughters, Pat and I wondered why they and their friends were becoming so aware of the opposite sex so early.

Then one day it came to us: television! Not just the majority of the programs but the *commercials* have been selling sexuality to children almost from the moment sets were invented. The commercials are often more interesting than the shows, and almost without exception they preach that the *highest goal in life is to acquire "sex appeal."*

Toddlers, sitting before television sets, have it drummed into their little heads over and over again, subtly and otherwise, that *their ultimate obligation is to attract the opposite sex.*

Well, Pat and I weren't pleased about this realization, but we didn't get terribly excited until we saw sex being sold through an *oatmeal* commercial. That's when Pat blew up. Sex with your breakfast food?

Try to visualize this, if you don't remember it: from the television set, during a break in some program, a voice implores us (and our daughters) to eat more oatmeal, and all the while on the screen, a terribly sensuous blonde in a bathing suit is licking a spoon. In a close-up, she dawdles over her oatmeal, licking her lips and running her tongue along the spoon's edge until the commercial looks like a scene from "Tom Jones."

Well, watching that, Pat got so angry that, when he spoke at an awards dinner for an advertising agency, he really laid them low. I imagine they were sorry they'd invited him, but the idea of promoting oatmeal through sex infuriated him until tact wasn't important.

Agencies advertising oatmeal aren't the only offenders, however. What about the commercial wherein the camera focuses on a can of hair spray while, in the background, slightly out of focus, a couple slides giggling onto a sofa and disappears? What conclusions does a child draw from that? *She may eventually conclude that her only guarantee for successful living is to use products which will make her sexually attractive.*

I'm convinced that our TV generation has gotten more than radiation from the tube. A society in which *Playboy* is one of the three best-selling magazines is sex-oriented to a destructive degree.

The other day one of Laury's little friends, a girl not more than 13, remarked that her life's ambition is to pose for the *Playboy* center fold, which seems to prove everything I've been saying. Women's Lib notwithstanding, millions of little girls have been brainwashed to believe that to be a sex symbol is womanhood's supreme calling.

So, all this being the case, Pat and I have given our girls "booster shots" to strengthen the protection against sexual license they received when they were "vaccinated" with knowledge of the devil.

In the first place, from the time our daughters were old enough to know what the word *date* meant, we've told them that they wouldn't be allowed to go out with boys alone until they were 16 years old. And, since they've grown up with this understanding, they've accepted it.

When Cherry had been dating for about a year I asked her, "Do you think you missed anything by not being allowed to date until you were 16?"

After thinking a moment, her answer was, "Nothing I wouldn't have wanted to miss."

In other words, she'd been spared facing the problems and decision-making her friends had to contend with when they were 13, 14 and 15 and already dating heavily. She watched them go through periods of jealousy, fights with their boyfriends, and all sorts of emotional crises before they were at all prepared to handle these things.

After Cherry started dating, she found herself in occasional situations which sent her running to me in tears. But, because she was slow to begin going out with boys, she was a little more mature, a little wiser, and a little better equipped to meet certain problems when they finally arose.

I know that gland-power can sometimes outmatch brainpower, even in the brightest, most level-headed teenagers, so I've urged each of my girls to put off her first kiss just as long as she can.

I don't tell her that kissing is immoral or unsanitary or anything like that, but I point out that a kiss is a very special mark of affection and, therefore, a girl's first kiss should be precious and memorable, not just a casual contact easily forgotten and signifying nothing.

By making our girls wait to date until they are 16—and by urging them to wait to kiss until their kisses will mean something enormously special, Pat and I believe we've given them one of the "booster shots" I mentioned earlier (administered with lots of love and togetherness!).

For their second "booster shot" we've given them plain, practical, straight-from-the-shoulder talk about the ills and downright stupidity of the so-called "new morality."

Some of the logic which seduces young people is as old as time.

The prevailing argument of a generation ago when people wore hats—"You wouldn't buy a hat without trying it on, would you?"—was probably a variation of Latin once effective in the top tier of the coliseum, "You wouldn't buy a toga, etc. . . ?"

While the plea, "Why should we wait when the bomb may drop on us tomorrow?" probably derived from a Dark Ages' argument, "Why should we wait when we may be killed by the Northmen (the black death, a dragon, etc., etc.)?"

On the other hand, boys and girls are currently being assailed by new and sometimes deceptively subtle attacks upon premarital chastity coming from surprising sources. Not only do certain celebrities openly flaunt their infidelities, their affairs and their unwed parenthood, but *some spokesmen for the church actually advocate sin!* Naturally they don't call it sin, but that's what it is just the same, if we can believe God's own Word.

In a recent story by Robert DiVeroli of Copley News Service, the Reverend William E. Genne, family consultant for the National Council of Churches, was quoted as saying that the family in American society will be strengthened by couples *living together for a time before marriage*, "to make sure their marriages will work."

Amazing, isn't it? A statement like this attributed to a churchman!

Confronted with such an argument stemming from such a widely respected source, it's small wonder so many young people sneer at the "Puritan ethic." Nor is it any wonder that parents who try to defend old-fashioned virtue often feel disarmed before they've begun to fight.

How can a mere mother answer the wisdom of the learned and ordained Rev. Genne? For that matter, how can she sell her old-fashioned conviction in contest with the glamorous life-style of certain jet-setters and movie stars?

Fortunately, I have two strong allies in my campaign to teach our daughters decency.

The first is an example. By looking around their own community, the Hollywood-Beverly Hills complex, they can see what happens to girls who abandon morality for pleasure or ambition. The entertainment community may not be more sinful than any other, but, thanks to eagle-eyed columnists, its transgressions are easier to examine. So by reading the papers (trades and dailies) and keeping their wits about them, Cherry, Lindy, Debby and Laury can observe the wages of sin.

A year or so ago, a beautiful young actress became the much-publicized mistress of a married man. They made no bones about their relationship, even though he had a wife and children. The actress's career was on the upgrade. I think she honestly loved her lover and thought he'd get a divorce and marry her.

As it turned out, he got his divorce, but he married someone else, while his discarded mistress, trying to restore her own ego perhaps, took another lover. Then another. She slept one night, not with one, but with two singers!

Now when columnists report her "dates," readers laugh; and when producers cast important pictures, they pass her by. Once a girl with great star potential, today she's become a joke to everybody, including her original seducer.

I've never discussed this particularly bleak Hollywood chapter with my daughters, but if they aren't aware of its unhappy heroine, they are aware of other girls whose careers have paralleled hers. They are aware of girls who, after dozens of interviews on "casting couches," suddenly realize that they've never gone before cameras and probably never will. Unwittingly, these girls have become unpaid prostitutes. These "models" and "starlets" drearily entertain actors and studio executives with free evenings.

I am very sorry for these girls. The example they set is a

telling argument in favor of chastity which, I pray, is not lost on other girls.

Where my own daughters are concerned, my second great ally in my campaign for old-fashioned virtue is, naturally, Pat.

As their dad, he has given the girls a man's point of view which most men still maintain—no matter how they lie to the girls they're out with![2]

Pat Boone Answers: What fathers should know best about "the new morality"

Dear Christian Dads:

In helping you help your teenagers deal with the sex temptations of our times I've decided the best way is to share with you how I've tried to help my own. Here is exactly the advice I wrote for them, Daddy to Daughter. I said:

In the first place, when you consider what sort of sex life you'll have (when considering living together outside of marriage), you have to decide whether you're going to accept or reject the Bible and its teachings. See, the Bible very clearly tells us that God intends each man to have one wife, for him to take care of her, and for the two of them to be true and faithful to each other.

In God's plan, a man and wife become as one flesh. You should no more divorce your mate than you'd remove half your body! So, if you *believe* that, and think of marriage as a permanent arrangement, you'll enter it only after you have given the step a lot of careful thought. Then, even in the face of temptations and in the unhappy times most couples eventually experience, you'll ask God to keep you faithful to your vows.

Unfortunately, though, most young people don't know

[2] Shirley Boone, *One Woman's Liberation*. Creation House Inc., Carol Stream, Ill., 1972.

God and don't consider their sex activities any of His business. Yet, even they should realize that living together without marriage is a mistake.

Look at it this way: You wouldn't consider going into a business venture with a partner, would you, without a contract of some kind? If you were going to commit yourself to a business deal, you'd want to be sure that your partner was going to commit himself, too, and that's why you'd probably insist that terms of the association be spelled out in a contract. At least, you sure *should!*

Way back, under the law of Moses, it was possible for a man to get rid of his wife by simply saying, "I divorce you." A woman, on the other hand, couldn't get a divorce. She was her husband's property.

Jesus was the only true Women's Liberator! He gave women new dignity and new rights. He not only forbade out-of-hand divorcement—the discarding of a wife simply because her husband was tired of her—but He told each husband that *his first earthly obligation was to his wife!*

Before the coming of Jesus, a wife was strictly at her husband's mercy—and I'm pretty sure no modern girl would want to revert to *that* arrangement.

I imagine that almost every girl today who enters into a sexual arrangement, or "trial period," does so with the expectation that she and her partner will live together as equals so long as their love lasts, believing that, if it ends, they can walk away from each other with "no harm done." In fact, trying to compare unlicensed sex with marriage is like comparing apples to oranges. They just aren't the same things at all.

Without a permanent commitment, there's little chance of a lasting relationship. Perhaps I can explain best with an example. The other night in Las Vegas I was washing my car, a Rolls Royce convertible, at an all-night station. I was washing it at night after my shows because the Las Vegas temperature was only about 110 degrees then, not 120 as it had been during the day.

A fellow working at the all-night station thought it was kind of funny that a guy driving a Rolls was washing his own car, but I said I liked taking care of it, and the two of us got into a conversation about how much we enjoyed caring for our automobiles. As we talked, I remembered something, and I told the fellow, "I enjoy this Rolls, but it's no prettier to me than a '50 Chevy Shirley and I owned when we first married and lived in Texas."

That Chevrolet (it was two-toned green with white sidewall tires) had about 80,000 miles on it. The tires were thin, and the seat covers were giving way. But it never needed a major overhaul. It was our car, Shirley's and mine, and we took good care of it because we knew that if anything happened to it, we'd be walking and riding the bus.

I'm sure other people didn't see the beauty in our car that I saw, but I loved it. It was my pride and joy because I'd put so much of myself into it. Its good qualities filled me with such pride that I didn't even notice the bad ones.

Well, I think that car can teach a lesson to every young couple planning to move in together without marriage. Without marriage, you won't see the good qualities in your mate that you would see if you'd committed yourself fully to the relationship. If, through marriage, another person becomes yours forever and ever and there's no easy way to walk off, you will give more of yourself to that person. You will be less likely to notice defects in that person and more likely to find the good qualities, because that person will have become *a permanent part of yourself.*

When I think of so-called trial marriages or sexual relationships without marriage, I visualize a supermarket where a guy can walk in, look over the goods, and sample whatever looks tempting before he buys.

He may open a can, take a few bites, and then put the product down, because something on another shelf looks more inviting. If a box of cereal tempts him, he opens the box, eats until he is satisfied, and throws the rest away.

Actually that's the kind of relationship young people

are advocating when they glorify trial marriage. Or "the new morality," as they call it.

They're pushing for a society wherein each person helps himself to a little of this and a little of that without buying a thing. Then, when he's had enough, he leaves the broken boxes and half-consumed products to the next shopper who may buy what's left and take it home or do a little more sampling and walk away *with no commitment to pay for anything.*

I don't have statistics on how many premarital relationships lead to anything permanent, but I'll bet you my Rolls that very few do. (I'd never bet that '50 Chevy!)

There can be no permanent relationship *until two people permanently commit themselves to one another!* One major feature of marriage is the lack of alternative.

I think the motion picture "Love Story" was basically destructive because it encouraged young people to move in together with the thought that everything is going to be beautiful.

As I said, a girl usually looks at a premarital alliance this way—romantically. She thinks (and probably the guy tells her), "We don't need a license. We'll just grow together and love each other."

Well, the guy may start out thinking that way, but, fair or not, he'll probably get tired of the restrictions and pretty soon he may have another affair on the side. Then gradually, and he'll find lots of reasons for this, he and the girl he lives with will have big problems and he'll move out, leaving her wounded and vulnerable. A perfect target for the next man.

I'm around these guys all the time and hear what they say, so I know what I'm talking about.

Even with a commitment like marriage, a couple will find it rough, very rough, to get through certain periods. And, if there's no marriage at all, it's irresistibly easy to give the whole thing up.

When young people ask, "But if we aren't happy

together, *shouldn't* we separate?" I say, "No." For not even the happiest of happily married couples have been happy every day of their married lives. Shirley and I can vouch for that!

But, with God's help, it's easier to stick to your commitment and work out your marital problems than it is to run away from them. In this connection I remember an actor who was an enormously popular star in the '30s and '40s, and whose wife was an important star until she retired following the birth of their now-grown children.

They'd been married for almost a generation when one day, about ten years ago, he announced, "Something's wrong. I'm not happy."

"What makes you think you are supposed to be 'happy'?" his wife, a sensible lady, replied smartly. "All you're supposed to be is doing your best."

Their marriage has continued. Though I can't guarantee how happy he is, I can almost guarantee that he's happier than he would have been if he'd left home in the pursuit of pleasure with a girl half his age.

I was on the "Virginia Graham Show" recently with an actress who told all the viewing world that her teenage daughter was living with a man and that, if things worked out, they would get married. The mother not only thought this was great, but other people on the show sort of went along with her.

Finally, Virginia asked me what I'd do if one of my daughters came to me and said she wanted to move in with some guy. I said, "Well, I'd ask her to come down with me to a quiet part of the house where we could have a talk. I'd tell her exactly how I felt about what she was planning to do, and then I'd turn her over my lap and spank the fire out of her."

When I said that, the audience erupted in a roar of applause. I got the feeling that the audience, at least, was wanting somebody to say just what I'd said: That, if a girl was thinking like a selfish child, she should be treated like one.

To return to the example of the supermarket. Every housewife who shops for her family's food knows how produce that's been handled a lot gets bruised, until nobody wants it.

The sexual smorgasbord, in which some of our young people are indulging themselves, will not only produce few if any lasting relationships; it will leave behind a debris of trampled emotions and broken lives.

When I see young men and women pairing off with others who have had one affair after another, I'm puzzled by their decision. Because I doubt that any one of them would want to be operated on by a brain surgeon whose past several patients had died on the table. Would you?

In other words, I'd rather be part of a *success story* than move in with the most beautiful girl in the world who'd been party to a string of brief love affairs.

I think of an apparently irresistible actress (no, I won't name her) who has married and divorced three times and who has been involved in who-knows-how-many other relationships, none lasting. And I have to conclude that, no matter how fascinating she is, there is something *basically lacking* in that girl. Why, I wonder, would anyone want to give himself to someone who is such a chronic loser?

If a wife has the "out" of divorce always available, it makes it easier for her to see the faults in her husband, and vice versa. A happy marriage isn't the easiest thing in the world to achieve, but it's much easier to come by than a happy-but-illicit affair.

In our house, sex is a good word! But we discuss sexual temptations openly as a trap set by the devil. Our daughters know that if they walk out from under the protection of God, the devil will quickly take over because he's always present and eager. But they also know that if they commit themselves to Jesus, He will bless them wonderfully. And most encouraging of all, He won't *let* them be tempted with more than they can bear.

2. A FALLEN WOMAN—AGE SEVENTEEN

Dear Mr. Boone:

I know you must be a very busy man; I don't even know if you'll ever get my letter, or be able to answer it. But I sure pray you will.

I pray you will bear with me and read my letter. I will try to explain as clearly and briefly as possible.

At the present I am studying in the Philippines as an exchange student. I have been here three months already. I am a 17-year-old teenage girl.

My father is a minister. I have moved often because of this, but I have never had trouble making friends because, I guess, I have an outgoing, daring sort of personality. By the time I was 13 years old it was obvious that I preferred friendship with boys rather than girls. I always seemed to get along better with boys than girls.

I have always had a boyfriend. From the age of 12 to 13 years old I went through the boy-chasing stage. Then from 13 to 15 I stayed the girlfriend of only one boy, though I did have another boyfriend who lived 600 miles away and I only saw him once a year when I went on vacation with my parents. My parents did not like me to have this serious relationship with one boy, and I often argued with my parents. More with my Mom than my Dad.

Then for about 6 months when I was 15 years old I played the game with a number of boys. Then I became very serious with one boy. Our friendship ended up as a sex relationship. This relationship lasted for about 2 or 3 months, until my father decided it was God's will to move churches.

Then this guy decided he had better find himself a new girl. We were the same age and he was good looking and a lot of girls liked him. During our relationship I started to drink (alcohol) and smoke. Also there was a constant fear that I would get pregnant, as we did not use any proper birth control. At one state (4 weeks before my family moved) I thought I was pregnant. He told me that if I did not kill the baby then he would die. The next day he became very ill. This really scared me and I prayed that God would kill my baby. The next day God let me know I wasn't pregnant. I know there are a lot of medical reasons other than being pregnant that caused my physical problems, but it nearly caused me to have a nervous breakdown. I know I would have had one if I hadn't looked to Jesus for help.

After moving with my parents I lost complete interest in boys. I was then 16 years old. I began to seek God more and more in my life. For the first time we became really close friends. I guess all my life I have been a Christian, but it was one of those up-and-down sort of Christian lives. This time I really wanted to trust God.

Then I received my scholarship to come to the Philippines. Again, I relied on God to guide my life and He did in so many wonderful ways. Not only before I came to the Philippines, but also after I came here. I read your book, *A New Song*, and I decided I wanted this new relationship with God. Both my parents have this relationship with God and I believe that after reading your book that I was baptized in the Spirit. But there were too many doubts in my mind and my faith was weak. But I know it happened.

A few weeks ago I went to stay at the home of a girlfriend, two sisters and brothers. Her brother took an interest in me and started to take me around town, especially at night. The fourth night at that home, I went with him and some friends, dancing and drinking at one of the many nightclubs there. I knew from previous experience that I have to drink a lot before I get drunk, and this night I drank just one mild drink. I was far from being drunk, but after the night club I let him take me to a hotel and have sex with me. During my two-week stay there we had sex a number of other times, the last time being last night. Every time I was sober and each time I knew what I was doing was wrong, but I couldn't stop myself. And for some reason I would not grasp hold of the strength God could give me. So last night to stop my guilty feeling, I let myself get drunk.

Please don't think I am proud of this because right now I feel so mentally and physically ashamed. I feel so sick inside and I guess you must feel sick just reading such a thing. I have never told my parents that I am not a virgin and I felt so ashamed when I read their letters filled with praise to God.

I'm now back at school and won't see my friend's brother for some time. I don't know if you know, but the Philippine moral standard for men is not very high. Most boys lose their virginity at about 16, and making love is just the natural thing. I don't love the boy, and in one respect I hate him.

I know God loves me and He has done so much for me, but still I "slapped Him in the face," so to speak. I really want to love God, because I know we can't live a happy life on this earth without Him.

I do hope you get my letter. I can't tell anyone else and there aren't many Christians here. The ones I do know I couldn't talk to about it. I pray you can help me in some way.

Please pray for me,
Connie

Dear Connie:

Your letter hit me hard, on a lot of levels. You know that I have four pretty daughters of my own and that I'm constantly trying to help them in their own tug-of-war with twentieth century morality. It ain't easy! Never was easy in any century—but I really think it's almost impossible for you young people to be moral and clean and truly loving today.

You're bombarded on every side, whether it's television or magazines or newspapers or movies (or even assigned reading material at school!), with strong influences to forget about "old-fashioned morality," and the Bible and church teaching, and "stuff like that." Politicians and movie stars and educators, business people, and even housewives are indulging themselves in whatever appeals to them. And psychologists are saying "I'm okay—you're okay," no matter what you are involved in. And many ministers are deciding that it's impossible to expect young people to stay moral and clean before marriage; so even they are trying to handle and explain away guilt, instead of helping young people chart a sane and considerate and healthful course through the difficult teenage years.

My heart really goes out to you, Connie.

I've written several books to teenagers about my own experiences, and the tussles that all young people have to face. My new book, *"A Miracle a Day Keeps the Devil Away,"* deals more fundamentally with this struggle with Satan than any book I've written before. That's what you're really involved in, you know. You are aware of that, aren't you?

What the psychologists and even liberal ministers don't tell you is that every time you satisfy a physical appetite in disobedience to one of God's "health rules," you contract a virus: sin! And every failure after that, every losing bout with this same deadly virus, leaves you in a more weakened position than before. The honest guilt you feel (because you *have* sinned) only makes things worse; Satan uses that to convince you that you aren't any good, that you're too weak to change, and that you might as well go ahead and indulge yourself as many times as you want to, because you're lost anyway.

Did you know that the Bible reveals him as "the accuser of the brethren"?

He's really good at that. You are one of God's children, and I believe that you have received His Holy Spirit, so that qualifies you as one of the devil's prime targets. And he will accuse you, and trap and involve and infect you, until he destroys you.

The apostle Paul was grappling with this same kind of elemental problem. If you'll read Romans 7 and 8 you'll see that even the Spirit-filled apostle of God was having some of the same struggles (though I doubt that he was losing as many battles). Read the seventh chapter of Romans, identify with Paul, and then read his exciting and dynamic prescription for success in the eighth chapter!

YOU DON'T HAVE TO BE A SLAVE TO YOUR OWN BODY AND APPETITE!

I shared with you in *A New Song* that all the answers to every one of my problems was supplied by Jesus as I totally surrendered my life and my will to Him.

I remind my very real enemy, Satan (and myself every day), that I want Jesus to control my life and to work in me "both to will and to work for His good pleasure" (according to Philippians 2:12-13). Think about that verse a minute. It allows me to put the burden on God to cause me to *want* to do His will—and then to *do* it. I really believe the Lord means what He says, and that He'll keep His promises!

Connie, please do a couple of things.

First, if you don't have one already, *please get a modern translation of the New Testament.* I suggest *The Living New Testament, Good New for Modern Man,* or the J. B. Phillips translation. All of them bring the Scriptures to life in words we can understand. It was a fantastic eye-opening thing to hear Jesus speaking to me in words that I use myself all the time. The truths are the same; they never change. Start to soak up these truths on a daily basis.

Now for a real challenge. It's obvious your malicious enemy, Satan, has wormed his way into your emotions, your senses, and even your thinking process. I think you know this and you've written to me for help. The devil doesn't want you to have it—and I'll guarantee he'll block it in any way he can.

So I suggest you do what Paul did in Acts 9:9: fast for three days, and pray just as often as you can during that time. If you have to work or go to school, that's all right. But try not to be around the people who would keep you drawn into this type of sin—dodge them if you can. It won't be easy. If I know Lucifer, he'll come at you in every way he can during that three-day period; he'll prompt some of your friends to find you wherever you are, and he may use them to tempt you with some of the strongest temptations you've ever faced.

He doesn't want to lose you!

But—if you're fasting and praying and reading the words of Jesus—you'll meet the test, and His Spirit will minister to you just like He did for Jesus.

Connie, if you will do this, the Lord will become so real to you; and so will your awareness of the supernatural struggle you're in with Satan; and by the end of the three days, you'll be excited about being on the winning team with Jesus!

Do you have the courage to enter into this kind of life-and-death scrap? If you do, Jesus Himself will be right in there with you—ready to prove His power and presence.

Connie, He loves you! He knows the desire of your heart, and God has promised to grant the desires of your heart if you delight yourself in Him (Psalm 37:4). God never promised that the Christian life would be easy because He knew that our enemy, the devil, is on the loose and will do everything in his power to keep God's children from enjoying a victorious life. However, we can praise God because Satan isn't nearly as powerful as God, and we have the advantage of the actual presence of the Holy Spirit in our lives. The power that created heaven and earth and that raised Jesus from the dead, is on your side to give you strength and victory.

Let me hear from you, Connie. And please take heart in this: YOU'RE NOT ALONE! Number one, every teenager in the world today is going through the same struggle. And number two, *Jesus Himself knows what it is to be a teenager*—He was there once, remember? He has special empathy for you, and will intercede for you in a very special way, if you'll just remember to keep calling on Him every day. And don't let our enemy, the devil, convince you that you can't win. With Jesus on your side—you can't lose.

I love you,
PAT BOONE

P.S. Connie, this may be very important: write or call your dad (God's spiritual covering for you), and without going into details, just ask him to double up on his prayers for you. I believe this will be very powerful spiritually.

3. SEX PROBLEMS IN MARRIAGE

Dear Mr. Boone:

I saw you on television where you said you prayed for people with problems. I have a very serious problem, one that I can't bring myself to go to a doctor about.

I am a 29-year-old mother of two. The problem I have is that I do not respond to my husband sexually. I've even tried to fake responding. This helps him at times, but does nothing for me. Sometimes when he touches me my blood seems to run cold and I'd rather he just not touch me at all. This problem has become so bad that the subject of separation has even come up. Any suggestions you may have would be greatly appreciated.

We've been married nine years and this is a nine-year-old problem.

There is perhaps more information about me that you need, but I don't seem to be able to decide what you'd need to know to help, so I'll just tell you some things about me.

I came from a poor family. At the age of 10 my parents got divorced because my father molested me. (I forgave him for this and I've prayed for God's forgiveness for him because he was, and may still be, an alcoholic.)

When I was in high school there was a very special guy named Gary. I was very serious about him, but in our junior year I broke up with him because we were getting real serious. I knew his plans for the future and I didn't want anything to keep him from having a chance for all his dreams to come true. Shortly after that I met Sam, my husband. We dated a lot. My mother and I never got along (we still don't), so I left home before I graduated from high school. Sam was always there when I needed him. He talked me into living with him, so I did. We lived together for almost a year. I felt guilty and didn't want to stay with him, but I was afraid to leave him; so I insisted that he either marry me, or I'd leave him. We were married and have had a good relationship, other than sexually. We seldom argue and when we do it's always about sex.

I care a lot for him and in my own way I love him deeply. Now it's not just two people, it's four, and our children deserve both a mother and father, so please help me.

I pray that you will answer my letter soon.

Thank you and God guide your answer,
Susan G.

Dear Susan:

Thanks so much for your letter. I want you to know that you are in our prayers and I know that our Heavenly Father loves you and has already sent His Holy Spirit to minister to your heart and give you His peace.

Jesus loves you, Susan, and He came to minister to the whole person and set you free from anything that would keep you from experiencing the abundant life He talks about in John 10:10. From what you have said in your letter, it seems that you have experienced more than your share of deep trauma and hurt. I'm sure you've forgiven the one who hurt you the most, but I'm sure too that there are still deep scars that you're not even aware of. This could be causing you to have some of the sexual problems in your marriage—simply because of the insecurity and fear it created. Some of these same reasons could be causing disharmony with your mother, too. God knows this—and understands!

I have good news for you, Susan! Jesus said in Luke 4:18 that He came to heal all the bruises and wounds and broken hearts that we experience, and He'll heal yours right now. May I suggest that you follow a little prescription that I think will help you experience the healing grace of Jesus? First, ask the Lord to reveal to you anything in your life, such as bad attitudes, unforgiveness, resentment or bitterness toward anyone. (That would include your family, husband, and even God or yourself.) Then make it right with God and possibly the persons involved, in other words, ask Him to forgive you.

Second, I would suggest that you forgive your mother for anything she may have done, either knowingly or unknowingly, that has caused your feelings toward her to be strained. If necessary, you may need to ask her to forgive you for some unthoughtful words or deeds on your part. The Lord will give you the strength to do this, and will work out the details of your future relationship with her. While you may never be in complete agreement with your mother in everything, the Bible says we are to honor our parents even in old age. Your mother must have suffered severe pain and emotional trauma during her marriage to your father, too, and no doubt needs to have the assurance of your love and forgiveness. And, of course, continue to have a forgiving and prayerful attitude toward your father.

You mentioned a former boyfriend you really cared for and with whom you broke relations in high school. I think the Lord would tell you that he is a thing of the past, and you shouldn't harbor any feelings of regret over ending that relationship. He was a stepping-stone in your growing-up process, and you can thank God for the experience, and move on to full appreciation of the man God intended you to share your life with—Sam. God brought you and Sam together, and has made you man and wife. It seems that you're still carrying a sense of guilt for living with him before marriage. And so, to free yourself of the guilt, just confess it to the Lord and ask Him to make your marriage a whole and complete one. He wants to give you both complete freedom and victory in every aspect of your marriage.

Most importantly, I hope you've been able to discuss

this problem with your husband. Be completely open about your letter to me and my answer. And, between the two of you, go to the Lord in prayer, committing yourselves individually and jointly to Jesus Christ. As you give your lives to Him, He'll bind you two together in a love like you've never known before. God will do it because He is love and His love will fill you and cover all the uncertainties and insecurities of the past, and especially release you from what it is that is keeping you from experiencing a complete and total freedom in your marital relationship. Trust Him, and just pour your heart to your Heavenly Father who will never fail you nor hurt you—but will give you the very best life has to offer.

Susan, I hope through prayer and reading the Bible that you'll learn to thank and praise the Father for all you're experiencing, because it's drawing you to Him for your answers and strength. Be sure to get involved in a good Bible-believing church and have fellowship with other Christian couples your age. Go to the pastor for prayer and counsel, and spend much time in personal prayer and Bible study. Trust God to use the Christians around you to help you in your need. Please know that we'll continue to hold you up in prayer, and I honestly believe that the Holy Spirit will come to you in a special way and fill you to overflowing with love for your husband, your parents, your children, and most of all for your Lord and Saviour—Jesus!

Your brother in Him,
PAT BOONE

4. ABORTION

Dear Pat Boone:

I'm in a terrible, terrible spot.

I'm 20 years old, unmarried, and pregnant. I think I love the man who got me pregnant, but I'm not really sure he loves me. He really doesn't want us to get married, and is trying to get me to have an abortion. I know it's legal now, and so many women seem to say it's okay. But I'm so mixed up, and I really don't want to do it if God or the Bible says it's wrong.

I don't have time to read the Bible and think about all this myself. I need answers. Can you help me?

Carlotta

This is typical of many letters I've received over the last several years on the same topic. As the father of four girls, and living in modern America, I had to really search my soul—and the Bible—to settle my own thinking on the topic of abortion. Here's my answer to Carlotta, and to my own daughters.

I know very well that it's a controversial theme, and there's much to be said on both sides. But from my own study and prayer and experience here's my answer.

Dear Carlotta:

I want to tell you first of something that happened in our household.

Our then 15-year-old blonde daughter had come home from school, trembling and depressed, tears right at the surface. Debby was really shaken. Badly. Naturally, Shirley and I wanted to know what was wrong.

She told us that she and a friend had wandered into the science lab during a free period, and had seen some new exhibits there. One of them was a large jar, with some strange object in it. They drew closer, expecting that it was some kind of pickled squid or other form of sea life, and to their horror, discovered they were looking at a human baby! The label said, "Two month fetus"; but Debby and her friend *knew* that they were looking at a well-formed, unborn child, with tiny ears and mouth and fingers and little curled up legs, with distinguishable toes.

And there it was, in their science lab, pickled in a jar like a cucumber!

Debby has never gotten over that experience, and neither have we. It has settled for all time, our feelings about abortion. That little child in the jar was well below the current legal limit for abortion, and hundreds of thousands of little ones like that are being scraped out of the wombs of America's women every year—thrown away like so much garbage.

I know it's a complex problem, and that women can argue with much emotion and some validity about their constitutional rights to privacy and control over their own bodies. As the one male in an otherwise all-girl house, I firmly believe in those rights, both constitutionally and ethically. But I also believe these rights should be exercised *before* pregnancy. And I certainly am all for abortion as long as it takes place before conception!

I and my daughters agree that, with the exception of rape, there is absolutely no reason that a woman can't exercise her right *and* responsibilities before she becomes pregnant. The most ignorant girl knows that sex produces babies, and the poorest women in America has access to the most effective contraceptive there is: the word "NO." Oh, I'm sure abortion advocates can come up with numerous exceptions to these general rules; but they are just that, *exceptions*. There is always a way for the thinking girl or woman to avoid pregnancy, if she thinks about it and accepts her responsibility and assumes her right *before* conception occurs. If only the millions of American women that are so energetically and militantly demanding their right on this issue would apply the same concern and effort toward preventing unwanted pregnancy, I'm sure the problem would be solved!

Okay, okay, Boone; you're talking about what should happen *before* conception. But what happens after the accident occurs?

Well, first of all, let's don't hide behind words like "fetus" and "abortion" and phrases like "embryonic sterilization." We're not talking about warts or callouses or cysts or other kinds of growths. We're talking about *life*. So let's also admit, when we're speaking of abortion that we're talking about *taking a life*.

I always base my answers to everything on The Manufacturer's Handbook, the Bible. And the Bible is very clear on this subject. Throughout that matchless book, God has made it plain that He personally takes a hand in every birth, and every vestige of life in His creation. Jesus said that His Father looks after every bird, and even every flower. He added that "you are far more valuable to him than they are"; and "the very hairs of your head are numbered" (Matthew 6:26 and 10:30). The prophet Isaiah, in a number of places, indicates specifically that God ordained and formed him (and others) in his mother's womb. The Psalmist David, in Psalm 139:13-17, says,

"Thou hast covered me in my mother's womb. I will praise thee; for I am fearfully and wonderfully made; marvelous are thy works; and that my soul knoweth right well. *My substance was not hid from thee when I was made in secret*, and curiously wrought in the lowest parts of the earth (or in the womb). Thine eyes did see my substance, yet being unperfect; and *in thy book all my members were written, which in continuance were fashioned, when as yet there was none of them!''*

Now, Carlotta, the Bible says that God is no respecter of persons. That means that He cares equally about each of us. And if He was watching over the very forming of David's substance while he was in his mother's womb, then He is just as concerned and involved with each of us.

When does life begin?

I know this is a crucial question, and there's been a lot of debate about it. But I look back to the first chapter of Genesis, when man was created. "And the Lord God formed man of the dust of the ground, and breathed into his nostrils the breath of life; and man became a living soul'' (Genesis 2:7). Now please follow this: After God had formed man, and held his body in His mighty hand, he was still just a beautifully formed blob of flesh, *until God breathed life into him!*

God has already breathed life into that creature forming within you now. That child is already growing, being nourished, is moving and shifting, is feeling and responding— and that's life! What a hideous perversion that we are accepting today (and it's only a fairly recent development) the unspeakable presumption of mere man stepping into God's place and chopping out and destroying a human being, and taking that infant's life into his own hands and ruthlessly throwing it away.

Carlotta, the problem is that in every area of life we are ignoring God and the Bible. It has become socially acceptable (and even recommended in many circles) to become adulterers and fornicators and murderers. In Galatians 5:19-21; Ephesians 5:3-5; Colossians 3:5-6, as well as 1 Corinthians 6:9-10, God says clearly that adulterers, fornicators, whoremongers and homosexuals shall not inherit the Kingdom of God! In fact, as He concludes His message (the Bible) to man He says in Revelation 21:8 that all whoremongers, and that means those who promote and indulge in sex outside of marriage, will join murderers and sorcerers and idolators and all liars, and unbelievers, in "the lake which burneth with fire and brimstone: which is the second death." I know that sounds harsh, but I didn't say it. God did—take it up with Him.

My point is that, in choosing to ignore God's specific instructions, we've not only set ourselves up for eternal destruction, we have created terrible problems in the here and now. Like unwanted babies by the millions. Like innumerable psychic and emotional scars. Like broken homes and warped, twisted relationships. Like abortion—and guilt by the world-full.

Abortion won't solve the problem of unwanted pregnancy, it will only compound it!

So what to do? May I give you a personal example? Shirley and I have had four healthy daughters, and for each one, we are deeply grateful. But we didn't plan on any of them, and in fact, were more than mildly distressed that they came as thick and fast as they did. Four in three and a half years! We thought we were taking precautions, but they came anyway! And Shirley had two miscarriages as well.

On top of this, Shirley's blood type is Rh-Negative. The doctors told us that Shirley should only have one or two children at most, and that after that there would be real danger to her and the potential offspring. But we prayed a lot, and committed these things to the Lord. Between the four healthy babies (miraculous, we felt) came one miscarriage, which we felt was God's wisdom. And *after* the four were born, when Shirley learned that *another* was on the way, she actually prayed that the Lord would spare her another birth so soon. She just felt she couldn't handle the pressure and stress of another child, with all the other responsibility she had right then.

Midway through the pregnancy, I took the family to England where I was filming, and while there Shirley lost that baby. The doctor told us later that it appeared deformed, and Shirley and I got on our knees to thank God for overruling in this situation. Are you getting my point, Carlotta?

You can't—or certainly shouldn't—undo what has already happened. But you *can* and should commit this to our heavenly Father, who "works *all* things together for our good, to those who love Him" (see Romans 8:28). I have discovered from my own experience that God's Word is true, and that He even works our mistakes together for our good, if we let Him. This thing is not in your hands now; it's in His, just as you and I are. Pray, Carlotta, and turn this whole thing over to Him.

If He permits you to go ahead and have this child, whether you marry your friend or not (and unless he begs you to, I wouldn't), if you don't feel that you can keep and raise the child, allow it to be placed for adoption, and pray that the Lord guide that baby to the right parents. My brother Nick, head of an adoption agency in Memphis, tells me that there is a much greater demand for babies than he and all the adoption people can meet.

I know this is tough advice, sweet lady, but there are three people involved here: you, your friend, and a human baby.

Have you ever read a partial list of the world's famous bastards? I mean people who were born out of wedlock, from illegitimate union, most of whom were totally unwanted at the time? Leonardo da Vinci, Alexander Hamilton, Charles Fremont, Ramsey Macdonald, John J. Audubon, Bernardo O'Higgins (Liberator of Chile), Alexander Borodin, Alexander Dumas, Cosima Wagner, and my dear friend, Ethel Waters. And just recently, in a San Diego paper, an old doctor friend of Marilyn Monroe's revealed that her parents had come to him and asked him to arrange an abortion, which he talked them out of.

Not long ago, on television, I saw a young man demonstrating in a right-to-life rally, carrying a sign which read, "Thanks, mom, for not flushing me down a toilet." There are hundreds of thousands of us alive right now who might echo that sentiment. Someday, Carlotta, the child you're carrying might say something like that to you.

One last thought. It occurs to me that even in this situation, Jesus can sympathize and identify with you. Remember, His mother, Mary, was in her middle teens when she discovered that *she* was pregnant and unmarried! The Father of *her* child wants to be your Father too, and the Father of your unborn baby. Under the circumstances, could you ask for anything better than that?

He's done the dying already; let Him show you what life is all about.

PAT

PART SIX: THE DEVIL'S CAULDRON

1. Witchcraft and Satanism
2. That Demon — Rum
3. Drug Addiction
4. Gay and Happy Aren't the Same
5. Fat, Fear, and Faith
6. A Cure for Television
7. Can We Win Against Pornography?

1. WITCHCRAFT AND SATANISM

Dear Pat:

I know you don't know me, but please don't let that stop you from reading this. I need your advice.

Maybe I should introduce myself. My name is Sara Green. I'm 21 years old. For three years I was a witch, but from there I went into Satan worship. I practiced black magic, drank blood and urine, ate flesh, praised Satan, and conjured up demons. Satan was my lord and I loved him. I had relations with animals for a while. I wanted to be a high priestess. I thought I could be one sooner if I destroyed your work. I read your book, *A New Song*, to find out where your weak points were. I didn't find any, but the book really affected me. I knew you were writing about something real, and I wanted it.

Well, after reading the book I wanted Jesus. My old associates knew and started threatening, so I moved. They hate Christians.

I tried to pray to Jesus, but it seemed like a civil war started inside. Gods argued inside of me. Demons showed up. I don't know what happened, but everytime I started to pray I couldn't. I can't figure anything out. I don't know why I can't pray.

I sometimes have suicide thoughts. I can't understand it, because I don't want to die. Can you help? Is there anything I should be doing?

I can't go inside a church. I usually get convulsions then. What am I doing wrong? Why can't I pray? Is there any hope? I'm writing sort of freely. I'd like to get everything out.

I know you get a lot of mail, so I don't know whether this will get to you or not. If you ever have time, though, could you maybe write? I'd really appreciate any advice.

Sincerely yours,
Sara Green

Dear Sara:

I'm very, very sorry that a month has gone by since you wrote me your letter. I was out of town with my family on a concert tour until barely a week ago. Since I've been gone almost six weeks, I'm much behind in my mail.

I'm quite sure, though, that the Lord heard your cry and has kept you safe until now. It may be that He's already answered your questions and drawn you into a warm Christian fellowship already. But in the event that He has given me the opportunity to help you, I want to give you my prayerful response to your letter.

What you felt as you read *A New Song* is real. This is the combined call of your own soul and of the Holy Spirit of God together. And, Sara, let me give you this encouragement: no power in heaven or earth, or under the earth, can overcome that team! Once your soul combines with the Holy Spirit in earnest desire, Satan himself and all of his legions cannot overcome you! Please read immediately Romans 8:31 through 39.

I hope you have a Bible nearby, and that you have access to a modern translation of some kind. I certainly recommend *The Living Bible*, or the *Good News for Modern Man*; in fact, I think I'll send one with this letter. God's Word is your most powerful weapon. Even when you don't *feel* anything, you can believe God to perform exactly what He says He will do. So it's very important that you have a Bible handy, and I would really recommend that you carry it with you all the time for a while. Remember: Jesus met Satan face to face in the wilderness (Matthew 4:1-11). He brought no weapon with Him except the Word of God! When He said,

"It is written . . ." three separate times, it was like bludgeoning Satan with an atomic hammer. The devil knows God's Word, and has to respect and obey it, when a believer speaks it.

Please read Ephesians 6:10 through 18. This passage tells us exactly what the nature of the battle is, and what our weapons are. You may not understand all of this right now, but at least I'm sure God will give you an understanding of the nature of the battle and how much He loves you and how He has already given you everything you need to win the battle. In fact, He's fighting on your side! Let your heart rejoice with this knowledge!

Did you ever see a tag wrestling match? This is when there are at least two wrestlers on each team, and only one from each team is allowed to wrestle in the ring at any one time. When one wrestler is getting badly beaten by his opponent, if he can just get back to his corner, or even close enough to reach out and touch the fingertips of his partner—in other words, if he can tag him—his partner can immediately leap into the ring, drag off the opponent who has the upper hand, and take over the battle himself! The partner who is being beaten can then get himself off the floor and outside the ropes and rest and recuperate, while his fresh strong partner takes up the battle.

Sara, we are in a tag team scrap with the devil and his angels. You have been out in the center of the ring, and in fact, over in the devil's corner, and have been getting the daylights beaten out of you. In fact, I guess, you didn't even know you were in a battle because you willingly joined his team. Now that you have begun to scrap, and have tried to get back into the other corner—he is certainly going to put up a fight, and drag you back if he can. He will use old friends, he will use his demons, he will accuse you and try to stand between you and Jesus in every way he can. The old suicide trick is one of his favorites. If he can't keep you willingly on his side, then he'll try to convince you that you've lost the battle, there's no reason to live, and that you should end it all. Then he's got you forever. Because you have allowed him to have control of your body, and get his hooks in you, he will exert every possible influence to keep you from touching Jesus. He has the ability to give you physical pain; emotional and spiritual obstacles; to work through friends and even family to block your path. He knows (even better than you or I) that if you simply reach out and touch the tip of Jesus' finger—he's had it! Jesus will come bounding over those ropes and scatter him right out of your life!

Here is the most important part of this letter: Read these verses in the tenth chapter of Romans. Begin with the verse 9 and read through verse 11. These verses simply say that Jesus is as near to you as your own mouth! To touch Him and bring Him into the battle, all you have to do is speak His name! As you speak His name, Jesus—which means "Jehovah is our salvation"—and believe in your heart that He is the Son of God, and ask Him to come into your life and to be your Lord and Saviour, He will. In verse 10, God Himself says that "with the mouth confession is made unto salvation." Can it be simpler than that? Satan himself cannot prevent you from speaking that name, receiving your salvation, and bringing Jesus and His Father into the battle for your life. Now read verse 13 and do it!

Don't put it off for even a second. The devil will try to stop you; he may threaten you physically, he may try to convince you that your heart will stop or your brain will explode or that your tongue simply will not speak that name. But, Sara, God is on your side, or I would not have received this letter. And you would not be reading this answer right now.

One last example. Remember the thief on the cross? Here Jesus was already nailed to the cross and His life's blood was draining away. On one side of Him was a thief who recognized that Jesus really was the Son of God. He was already nailed to a similar cross for his own sins. Even in that lost, dying, and hopeless situation, he simply turned and spoke to Jesus and recognized Him as the Son of God. Jesus turned and said to him, "Today you will be *with me* in Paradise." Your situation cannot be as hopeless as that poor thief on the cross. And Jesus saved him and took him that day to Paradise! Isn't that thrilling? This is in Luke 23:39-43, in *The Living Bible*.

Sara, I'm praying right now that Jesus will get this letter to you quickly, that He will make the Bible available to you, and that He will bring Christian friends into your life who have the power and the knowledge of the Holy Spirit operating in them. I believe He will do this. Will you cooperate by doing a strange thing? Will you fast—go without food—for a day or two or three? In the fourth chapter of the little book of James, God says in verses 7-8 that if you resist the devil, he must flee from you. He also says that if you will draw near to God *He will draw near to you!* One of the very best ways to draw near to God is to deny your flesh, to actually go without food for a time and let every hunger pang be a silent prayer for the Lord to draw near to you. He will! Jesus actually fasted for 40 days before He met the devil in that big showdown. None of us could do that; but if you will make that your prayer for a day or two or three, I earnestly believe that the Lord Himself will bring into your life Spirit-filled believers who will minister to you, and take you out of the influence of Satan and those that he still dominates. Do not believe that you can't pray! Your letter itself is a prayer. Your fasting will be a prayer. And every word you speak that is directed to the Lord is a prayer. Don't believe that because you don't *feel* you're getting through that you're not. You *are*—this letter proves it!

One last Scripture in this spiritual prescription: read Lamentations (in the Old Testament between Jeremiah and Ezekiel), the third chapter, verses 22-28. Also verses 40-41. These are a description of where you've been, but also of the goodness and ever-ready mercy of God. He loves you and is already working to answer the prayers that you didn't think were getting through! Be happy, Sara. I'm praying for you now—and I know that the Lord has already engineered your salvation and a life of happy relationship with Him. Write me the good news.[3]

In the love of Jesus,
PAT

[3]Pat Boone, *A Miracle a Day Keeps the Devil Away.* Fleming H. Revell, Old Tappan, N.J., 1974.

2. THAT DEMON—RUM

Dear Pat Boone:

I am a girl of 24, a mother of one girl, and a housewife. I am an alcoholic. If my husband knows, he's not letting on.

The reason I am writing is because I believe your story. If the Lord God and Jesus Christ see fit to answer your prayers, *would you pray for me to see the light!* Take me out of the dark. I feel like a four-legged animal.

Please pray for me. This is not a crackpot letter—I'm in earnest. I'm sure the Lord will give you a feeling when you read this that I'm sincere.

From a faithful friend, with love,
Karen Johnson

Dear Karen:

Your letter has reached me and I do feel that God has taken a real interest in you and in your problems and that He will provide the answers.

I'm sending you a couple of books that I hope you'll take the time to read immediately. One is *Face Up With a Miracle* by Don Basham, and the other is *Run Baby Run* by Nicky Cruz. Both of these people are dynamic friends of mine, but they both had problems that only God could solve. Please read them right away and let me know your reaction.

Also, if you don't have one already, please get a *Living New Testament*. It's called just that, and you can get it in paperback in the local bookstores. I really believe that God will speak to you as you get that Bible and begin to read the words and the promises and the compassion of Jesus. In the meantime, I'm praying that the Lord will take a firm hand in your life right now, and will rebuke your enemy, Satan, who is continually whispering in your ear that you need the very thing that will destroy you. So many people today think that Satan is some kind of myth—and how he loves for us to believe that! He is just as real as God Himself. And God says so! And he knows just how to make slaves of each of us if we let him; and he finds it especially easy if we don't even recognize his tactics. When you feel that old urge and that old craving, realize that it is Satan himself doing his best to trap and destroy you. From what you say, so far, he has been having a field day. No more! From now on you and God can rebuke him and in the words of Jesus say, "Get thee behind me, Satan."

Jesus is nearer to you right now than your own breath—trust Him. Talk to Him. Believe that He will help you now.

Your Christian Friend,
PAT BOONE

Dear Pat:

I can't begin to tell you how I felt when I first received your letter, Mr. Boone. As usual, I wept. I don't know why, but I couldn't write back for some time.

A week after I wrote to you, I was committed to an alcoholic rehabilitation rest home. I stayed for two weeks under medication, good food, rest and company of my own kind. I haven't touched a drop in three months. But I'm still not happy. Please, Mr. Boone, don't give up on me. Your prayers, combined with my mother's, delivered me from alcohol; now the devil has found other ways to torture me. Where one path was closed, another opened.

I came from a very stormy background. I found comfort in food and naturally I became obese. Stormy or not, we did go to church every Sunday and my one prayer to God was "please make me slim and let me find a good husband." My prayer wasn't answered overnight, but by my late high school years I discovered I was downright pretty, with a good figure and lots of boyfriends to choose from. I had fun, worked after school and had plenty of dates to keep me busy. And I met my husband by the end of my senior year.

But, Mr. Boone, I abused my gift. I became vain and stupid, lazy, and I drank! Now, after the drinking stopped, I am a foodaholic again. A potentially obese person. An obese person eats like an alcoholic drinks.

I just don't know what I'm doing wrong. I read your books, the Bible and others on my own. I've prayed for strength, but for some reason this stupid devil won't leave me alone. He plagues my heart and he plagues my mind, and he plagues my body. All I do is eat and cry, but I don't drink.

I wasn't going to bother you again, but I know you can help me. It says in the Bible in Mark 16:17 that you can cast the devil out of me. So I shall be like the woman Gentile who pestered Christ until He was moved by her faith and healed her daughter.

Perhaps this is out of line, but I love you for your interest and concern, and also thank God for you. I believe in Christ, but something's wrong—but it's me, not Him.

Thank you for your help,
Karen Johnson

Dear Karen:

Your letter moves me deeply and fills me with an excited expectation. Jesus has heard your prayers and is answering them just as surely as He did Cornelius in the tenth chapter of Acts. I'm certain that He brought you to just the right hospital and compassionate care that you needed. I'm also certain that He prompted you to read my book and to write me, and saw to it that I got your letters and had time to answer. Romans 8:28 is at work in your life as surely as you're reading this letter.

You mentioned that although you have now read and

believed with your mind and your heart that Jesus is surely the Son of God and that He does work in our lives and that He can free you from these attacks and enslavements of Satan, there is still something missing and you don't have the power that you need. Karen, what you need is the power of the Holy Spirit in your life. Jesus told His disciples, just before He ascended, to go into Jerusalem and wait until they received power. He didn't want them to try to go out and teach the good news and share the gospel and be His ministers under their own steam. He wanted to dwell in them and to give them the same power that He had as He walked the earth in the flesh. He said many times that His power came to Him from God by the Holy Spirit. He also said in John 14, 15 and 16 that He wanted His disciples to have this same Holy Spirit, and that by His Spirit He would dwell in them. And in you!

You mention this conflict that still rages in your body and mind, and you recognize that the devil is doing his best to pluck from you what the Lord has so generously given you. Please read what Paul says in Romans 7 and 8. Please read both chapters because they outline the terrible fight that goes on in the average Christian and even in the apostle Paul. He says, "When I want to do good, I don't; and when I try not to do wrong, I do it anyway. Now if I am doing what I don't want to, it is plain where the trouble is: sin still has me in its evil grasp. It seems to be a fact of life that when I want to do what is right, I inevitably do what is wrong." *There is only one way to be victorious*—by the indwelling of Jesus' Spirit. Paul asks the question like this: "Who will free me from my slavery to this deadly lower nature? Thank God! It has been done by Jesus Christ our Lord. He has set me free." And He will enter you and set you free if you ask Him to. This is what you must do immediately if you haven't done it already.

Just read Jesus' promise in Luke 11 that He would give the Holy Spirit to those who ask. And then in your desire for

Him and His fullness, and in your awareness of your desperate need and your inability to withstand Satan's attacks on your own, even with all the knowledge and the belief that you have—cry out to Him and express your need in whatever sounds come to your lips. Let your own voice and lips express the desperation in your soul, your longing for Jesus and the desire that you have to know His unspeakable joy. The Bible says that God knows what we have need of *before* we ask! He knows our thoughts and needs and yearnings better than we do ourselves! So what difference do the puny words that our minds can form really make? What really matters is what your heart desires, and the fact that we earnestly ask God to enter and take control through Jesus our Lord. Do that, Karen, and I guarantee you that the devil must leave you! Oh, he'll bother you again and continually try to rob you of this precious gift; but when you have asked Jesus to dwell in you and to reign over your heart and soul, then you can claim the promise "Greater is He that is within me than he that is in the world" (see 1 John 4:4).

God bless you, and I hope you will let me know of your triumph in Jesus.

Your brother,
PAT BOONE

3. DRUG ADDICTION

Mr. Boone:

Please excuse, and by so doing, also accept this letter, in light of its informality, but acute and deep sincerity. This, together with my 'convictions, background, education and own personal "up-hill" battle, lead me to write you, not even knowing if you even open or read such mail. I am, however, somehow convinced it will reach you and be evaluated by you (hopefully personally).

I am, firstly, an active member of a church, holding high offices. I am secondly, a family man, with two sons and a lovely, deeply devoted and deeply motivated wife. We have been married, and extremely happy for 15 years (excepting for about three just-past years). I am thirdly, a registered pharmacist, and I am lastly, currently involved in the total self-mastery I must achieve over drug addiction. This is the reason for three years of marital unhappiness; not divorce, but temporary separation and deep and total infliction of pain, loss of trust, abuse of trust and repeated and numerous "pick-me-ups" only to become "fall-me-downs" on my part.

As a result, I now have extreme difficulty in obtaining work in related fields, as I have voluntarily prohibited myself from practicing pharmacy for close to a year now.

Mr. Boone, I know as you do, I'm sure, the scope of drug abuse (both illegal and "legal") and all that accompanies it—from "bottom-rung" losers to halfway houses, to "sophisticated" organized hospitals. The scope of drug addiction knows not age, color, sex, culture, ethnical, ethical and economical backgrounds nor boundaries whatsoever! We know it has "all of the great people" by the throat like an iron-tight vise and is not yet, sadly, ready to even loosen up a bit.

So, Mr. Boone, a suggestion, a direction, a hint or information is what I ask. I know people and groups of all ages since I have held teaching and administration positions in churches and professional circles. I am not wealthy and not yet cured in my problems sufficiently to return to my profession, but hopefully I will be able to soon. Please write if at all possible, and I thank you deeply for forthcoming effort and for all you are doing now and have done for your fellowmen, therefore for Jesus!

Very sincerely,
Jim Parker

Dear Jim:

I have put off answering this letter for a few days so I could think and pray about it. I earnestly believe that you are right in feeling that somehow God motivated your letter and that somehow we are linked, at least by correspondence, for His glory and for His direction in your life. So I didn't want to just sit down and dash off a shallow note. Please bear with me now.

I have a couple of specific things to urgently recommend. If you haven't already read them, please buy and read David Wilkerson's *The Cross and the Switchblade*, Nicky Cruz' *Run Baby Run*, and my own book, *A New Song*. These books are similar in at least one very important aspect. Each of them is a true story about a man with a desperate problem. David Wilkerson as a young man went into the ghetto areas of Brooklyn to try to help thousands of kids with drug and violence and sex problems. He had to have miracles from God to accomplish anything, and God really backed him up.

Nicky Cruz was one of the first converts in Wilkerson's ministry, and was known as "The Garbage Can Killer" of

Brooklyn. I know both David and Nicky and I know that these stories are true in every detail. I really think they can be a tremendous help to you.

The third book is my own story, and I too was a man with desperate problems. This is what the "new song" is all about. I was looking for the very things you are—God's help with my problems, and real and new direction in my life. Jim, I earnestly believe that these three books can be used of God to suggest the answers in your life. Please get them and let me know your reaction.

You mentioned that you're involved in total "self-mastery." Jim, with all the fervency in my spirit let me assure you there is *no such thing*. Praise God, we are not meant to be masters of ourselves! We are meant to be slaves to Christ, His absolute bondservants. As you know, the Bible says, "It is not in man that walketh to direct his steps." Paul said, "I can do *all things through Christ who strengtheneth me.*" Philippians 2:12-13 gives us the formula for victory in our lives—"Work out your own salvation with fear and trembling, for it is *God working in you* both to will and to do His good pleasure!"

Too many people in this world, especially devout religious people, are trying to please God with their own efforts and to solve their life's problems under their own steam. It cannot be done. Read the seventh and eighth chapters of the book of Romans, and if you don't already have the modern translation, *The Living New Testament*, please get it. In these two chapters Paul outlines his continual grappling with problems that simply were bigger than he was. And he gives the only solution to these problems, the absolute mastery of the Holy Spirit in our lives. Jim, we have discovered this is not an intellectual concept and that the Holy Spirit does not rule us simply through our minds. He has to have control of my spirit and my soul as well as my mind and body. I really believe that *The Living New Testament* translation will help everything to jump to life in your mind and help you to be able to experience the victory that you're looking for. It has been invaluable to me.

What I'm really trying to get across is what Paul says in Ephesians 6:1-18, and I won't quote this, but again ask that you read it from *The Living New Testament* for its full impact. Too many people for too long have thought that victorious living and salvation itself came from belonging to the right group and from depending upon the "right people." I struggled along this way for thirty years myself. The answer that I have now experienced is summed up by Paul in the first four verses of Romans 8, and it is absolutely beautiful. The burden is not on you; Jesus Himself will take the burden if you let Him. I pray that you will, Jim, and that what may sound like Greek at this point will be quickened by the Spirit of God as you read these things and ponder them in your heart.

I know that the Lord has prompted your letter and my answer, and now we leave it in His hands.

Another servant of Jesus,
PAT BOONE

4. GAY AND HAPPY AREN'T THE SAME

Dear Pat Boone:

I have read your book and nothing has ever hit me quite so hard. You see, my problem is unusual, although being in the entertainment world, you've probably run across it.

I am a female who belongs to the gay world, and what I do at this point very definitely affects another person.

Although I had a very devout and religious attitude when I was younger (against my parents' wishes), I became very fond of a lady high school teacher. Then in my junior year an older man whom I had been dating regularly suddenly showed up in church with his wife. I was completely broken and fell back upon my teacher friend.

The summer before I entered college this friendship developed into a homosexual relationship. I went through six or seven periods of moving in and out because my friend was concerned over our age differences (21 years). This did not deter me. Earlier when I had been in close connection with the church, I prayed that God would let love come to us. At that time, I could see no wrong—now I honestly don't know.

I have not attended church anywhere regularly. I am a music teacher and love my work. By the way, I'm also a singer of sorts, and that's one of the ways in which I have been involved in the church. I have a few students who take private lessons with me, and I have encouraged them to participate in church activities.

Well, I'm not giving you my good side against my bad side. I just can't seem to sort things out properly. I am a 27-year-old graduate student, but I can't answer these questions. What hope is there for me? Can I continue to love another woman whom I practically compelled to love me? Does God say there is one and only one way to live?

I felt if anyone would know where to seek help, you would. I know I should go to God, but I'm so afraid. It could mean a change in my way of living, and that could destroy someone else's life. You see, one of our gay group had some kind of religious experience and now she lives alone.

My friend has read your book and knows I'm upset. But, we've both read similar accounts. *This just got to me.* I've tried to convince my friend that my love is still the same, but I haven't even convinced myself.

By the way, we are not the carousing, bar-hopping type. We lead a very quiet life and have a few other gay friends, but still I don't know what could happen. I guess somehow I hope that God can accept me and let me remain with my roommate.

I don't know what else to tell you. You may consider this letter a waste of your valuable time. I hope not.

Of course, due to the situation at home and my very private life against my very public life, please send anything in care of General Delivery. You may not even wish to answer, but after reading your book, I had to write. I'm so confused even rereading my letter.

Hopefully,
Joy Carol

Dear Joy:

Your letter has really had an impact upon me. I've had other letters from men and women with similar problems, but I really detect in you an earnestness and an honesty and a genuine desire to be in the center of God's will. I know that He has heard your request and knows your heart and will draw you perfectly to Him. I think the fact that your letter got to me is just one indication of the way He's working in your life.

As I was reading it a Scripture verse came to my mind. I looked it up and found it in Deuteronomy, chapter 30, beginning with verse 11. I think it would be good to read from there on to the end of the chapter, but the special passage that came into my mind was in verse 14, "But the word is very near you, *in your mouth and in your heart*, that you may do it."

Throughout your letter there is the indication in your own words that you realize something is wrong, out of kilter, not in balance in your life, and you're wanting very much for your life to be close to God and ordered as He would have it.

Now jump into chapter 10 of Romans beginning with verse 8 and read through verse 11 or even into verse 13.

(Notice that Paul was familiar with this spiritual principle that Moses had written in Deuteronomy, and he brought it right up to date and into the Christian time there in chapter 10 of Romans.)

Verse 10 is especially important to you: "For with the heart man believes, resulting in righteousness; *and with the mouth he confesses, resulting in salvation.*" That spiritual principle is just as alive today as when Paul first uttered it, and it's already operating in your life! It has caused you to write the letter; it has caused the letter to get to me; and now my answer comes back to you. But the best part is that *God has known the desire of your heart* and is honoring the confession of your mouth.

Joy, I'm not a preacher, and I'm no great Christian. I'm just a human being who has come to understand a little bit of God's love and power for us today.

I want you to know that I do not judge or condemn you in any way. As you already read in my book, I slipped into all kinds of sin and it nearly wrecked my life. I thought I had good reasons for it, and a lot of it seemed harmless and even very good for me and the other people involved. But gradually, like a cancer, it was destroying everything that was really precious to me and making it impossible for me to function as I was meant by God to function—and therefore robbing me of the only real happiness that there is in this life.

As you already read, I found that all the answers to every one of my problems was supplied by Jesus as I totally surrendered my life and my will to Him.

I have to repeat this process every day and remind myself and my very real enemy, Satan, that I want Jesus to control my life and to work in me "both to will and to work for His good pleasure" (according to Philippians 2:12-13). That last verse has become very exciting to me now because it allows me to put the burden on God to cause me to want to do His will—and then to do it. He says He will, and He will!

May I suggest a couple of things?

First, if you don't have one already, please get a current version of the New Testament. I suggest *The Living New Testament, Good News for Modern Man,* or *The New Testament in Modern English* (Phillips' translation). All of them bring the Scriptures to life in today's language. It really was a great breakthrough to hear Jesus speaking to me in words that I use myself all the time. The truths are the same; they never change.

The second is a rugged one. I believe our malicious enemy, Satan, has gotten quite a grip on your emotions, your senses, and even your thinking process. You have felt this and cried out for help. He doesn't want you to have it and *will block it any way he can.*

So I suggest you do what Paul did in Acts 9, verse 9: fast for three days, praying just as often as you can during that time. If you have to work, that's all right, but try not to have any company at all with the people who would keep you drawn into this gay world. It won't be easy. If I know the devil, he will tempt you in every way he can during that three-day period, causing some of your friends to find you wherever you are, and to tempt you with perhaps the strongest temptations you've ever faced.

But if you're fasting and praying and reading the words of Jesus you'll be strong, and His Spirit will sustain you. At the end of that three days I believe that you will come to recognize your enemy and also to have a very keen sense of the presence of the Lord with you.

Do you have the courage to enter into such an elemental struggle as this? If you do, Jesus will be with you.

Joy, sweet sister, our enemy is real! It is not your love for your friends—male and female—that is wrong and destructive: it's the sensual element that Satan has woven into it, taking advantage of mutual weaknesses and mutual emotional scars and twisting them into something destructive to you and to your friends.

Jesus won't ask you to give up your love for them; but He will purify it and make it constructive and helpful for their sakes, for yours and for His own sake.

You see, He died for your friends just as He died for you and me, and He loves them and perhaps will help them eternally through you. You can't help them, no matter how much you may want to, but He can, and will. Read Ephesians 6, beginning with verse 10 and through verse 17. You're in for a battle, so you might as well know the nature of it and the weapons at your command. Also read James 4, beginning with verse 7 through verse 10. This is a blueprint for action and a battle plan for victory.

I also believe that before that three-day period of fasting and prayer is over the Lord will have brought someone to you who can be a continuing source of spiritual strength. I have no idea who it will be, but He does. Test Him; try Him; let Him prove to you personally and intimately how wrapped up He is in your life and how well He knows your needs. This will be the most exciting adventure of your life, Joy.

Meanwhile, I'll be praying for you and claiming the victory that I know God will bring into your life if you'll just turn it over to Him. Thanks for writing me and for giving me the opportunity to share in this adventure that you have already begun.

Your brother in Jesus,
PAT BOONE

(This letter from Joy naturally started a series of letters through which she was brought out of the desperate confusion she was experiencing into a life of real "joy" and peace of mind. Because of the nature of the correspondence we thought it would be helpful to share it with others who might be confronted with a similar problem. We put all of our letters together, and a book was born.[4])

[4]Pat Boone, *Joy—A Homosexual's Search for Fulfillment.* Creation House Inc., Carol Stream, Ill., 1974.

5. FAT, FEAR, AND FAITH

Dear Mr. Boone:

I have read your book, *A New Song*, and got great strength from it. I do need you and your family to pray for me, though. I'm very confused and lonely.

My name is Sandra Culp and I'm 25 years old. I'm quite overweight and cannot control my eating alone. I've been quite plagued by problems in my lifetime. My parents are separated and have been for as long as I can remember. All my life they have given me anything I could ask for—within reason, and as a result of this, I feel insignificant and very inferior. I lost a lot of weight when I was about 15, but when I was 17 my parents' situation exploded because my father was and is now seeing another woman.

The town I'm from has only about 15,000 people and my father is very well known there. He began driving his girlfriend around openly, and I, as well as my friends, would see this and I became very upset and embarrassed.

I began to eat, and when my mother would tell me to stop, I'd sneak around and eat twice as much. Thus I gained over 100 pounds and now weigh a disgusting 235 pounds. I'm only 5 feet, 3 inches tall and it's miserable.

I have several beautiful friends, but they're all thin and can't actually understand my problem.

I have a pretty good singing voice, and for a while I wanted very much to pursue a career in music, but I think the thing I want more than anything else is a husband and family. I have so much love inside me and no one to give it to! I feel my voice is best used in praising God.

I have prayed to God several times to ask Him to take my life and guide it in His will, but I don't hear His answer. I've also asked Him to give me the strength to lose the 125 pounds I need desperately to lose. But I feel like He doesn't hear me. Can you and your family, who are so close to Jesus, ask His help for me?

I need help desperately because I'm about to lose all faith in everything, and I'm afraid.

Please help me!

Thank you and may God hear you,
Sandra Culp

Dear Sandra:

Your letter touches me in an unusual and deep way.

This is surprising, since I've never had much of a weight problem myself. Almost everybody else in my family (all girls, as you know) *is* dieting from time to time, and so I'm constantly aware of what a problem this is for many people. In fact, I guess the problems of diet and excess weight must be common to more people in America than almost anything else.

I think that's why your letter has hit me so hard. As the saying goes, "where there's smoke there's fire"—and where so many millions of people have this same problem, there must be something very basic about it, and probably a spiritual solution. The more I've thought about answering your letter, the more these three words have come into focus: FAT, FEAR and FAITH. I believe the three are very intimately related.

Isn't it interesting that Satan's first temptation of man, and the one that led directly to his downfall, was to eat? I believe the Genesis account, and in Genesis 2, God commanded Adam, "From any tree of the garden you may eat freely; but from the tree of the knowledge of good and evil you shall not eat, for in the day that you eat from it *you shall surely die.*"

Get this, Sandra; eating and disobedience equal death. Eating and faith equal life. Eating itself is not destructive, because God provided all kinds of great things for Adam and Eve to eat. But Satan knew that coupling disobedience with gratification of the flesh would lead to man's destruction, and it did.

Isn't it also very interesting that this same Satan, when he had the chance to face Jesus one-to-one and take his best shots, tried to get Jesus to *eat?* In Matthew 4, Satan, knowing that Jesus was hungry, said to Him, "If you are the Son of God, command that these stones become bread." In other words, "You have a fleshly desire, don't you? Well, what's wrong with that? Go ahead and satisfy it—eat."

It would have seemed to most people a very logical suggestion, and most of us would have jumped at the chance, wouldn't we? But Jesus saw that the devil was trying to work through the appetite of His own flesh to bring about His destruction. So He answered Satan with the Word of God, "It is written, man shall not live on bread alone, but on every word that proceeds out of the mouth of God."

There is such a deep spiritual principle here, Sandra. And I see that it runs through the Bible from Genesis to Revelation. Esau sold his birthright to Jacob to satisfy his hunger. The children of Israel disobeyed God in the wilderness because they wanted more than manna, and they were afraid that they wouldn't be satisfied. We are now creatures of flesh, and our tendency is always to satisfy the demands and cravings of our bodies, no matter what the consequences later.

I'm sure that's why Jesus set a new principle in motion beginning with His face-to-face meeting with the devil. Knowing that He was going to have this showdown, and that His spirit needed to be in control—not His flesh—*He fasted forty days!* Imagine going without any food for forty days! But do you see the reason for it? The more Jesus separated Himself from the cry and craving of His flesh, the stronger He became in *spirit*, and the more distinctly He could hear the voice of God. As a result, though Satan felt he was coming up against a weakling, he walked right into a spiritual buzz saw. Jesus really chopped him up!

I'm sure that's why Jesus recommended fasting for all of us, and that His disciples in the first century fasted a lot. They knew that by denying the craving of the flesh, they could bring back into balance the body, soul and spirit.

You realize that these are three separate parts of every human being, don't you, Sandra? Paul said in First Thessalonians 5:23, "Now may the God of peace Himself sanctify you entirely; and may your *spirit and soul and body* be preserved complete, without blame at the coming of our Lord Jesus Christ." To illustrate this truth, imagine three circles; one the size of a fifty cent piece, inside that circle another the size of a quarter and inside that a third circle the size of a dime. The outer circle is the body; the middle circle is the soul; and the innermost circle is the spirit.

Here's the most important part of this letter, Sandra: most folks want to tackle the problem of fat starting on the outside. Very few ever succeed. I suggest that you tackle this problem on a spiritual level, by allowing God to work *from the inside out!*

This reminds me of something the fat comedian said once, "Inside every fat person, there's a skinny person trying to get out." I really believe that's true. You are a thin, attractive and healthy person—imprisoned in 125 pounds of extra flesh. Well, Jesus came to liberate captives (Luke 4:18), and He could do it because, as He said, "The Spirit of the Lord is upon me"! That is, He and His Father were communicating freely on the spirit level, and therefore Jesus could approach every human problem at its spiritual core.

He's still doing it just that way.

Sure, you've had a lot of emotional and physical problems, and these are the superficial cause of your eating and overweight. But those are just the soul and body levels.

What about the spiritual level? You give me a very distinct clue in your own letter when you say, "I began to eat, and when my mother would tell me to stop, I'd sneak around and eat twice as much." It was then that you gained over 100 pounds and your weight zoomed to 235.

Can you see a parallel between that and what happened to Adam and Eve? Can you see that the excess weight (and your eventual physical destruction) is linked with disobedience? Can you see why I link fat, fear and faith? I really believe that the final solution to your problem is a spiritual one.

In Philippians 2:12 Paul urges us to "work out your own salvation with fear and trembling." This sounds awfully difficult, almost impossible, unless you go ahead and read the next verse, "For it is God, *working in you*, both to will and to do His good pleasure!" Think about that a lot—God working *in you* (on the spirit level) to change your *will* and help you to *do* His good pleasure. And what is His good pleasure for you, Sandra? I'm sure that His good pleasure for you is that you be lean and well and attractive and happy.

So I have a couple of very concrete suggestions. I'm not writing any diet books, but I do believe it's a sound scriptural prescription for the problem you face. First—fast. That means go without any food whatsoever, for a prescribed period of time. In the beginning, it might be half a day; or a day. If you feel up to it, I would suggest at least a whole day, maybe two, at the most three.

And I don't mean just do without food; I mean to turn every hunger pang into a prayer, and focus your whole being—body, soul and spirit—on the Lord, who is the source and the wellspring of your happiness and your satisfaction and your fulfillment. As you fast, I would suggest that you use your pretty voice and sing every song you can think of to express your devotion and gratitude and your need to the Lord.

Don't look for a big weight loss during the period of

fasting. I really don't expect that your flesh will be affected much during that period (though it may be), but your spirit will be strengthened greatly!

And the second suggestion is that you cram as much of God's Word in as you can! After forty days of fasting, Jesus preferred God's Word to bread; He knew that's where the real nourishment and satisfaction was. Oh, He loved to eat; later on He was accused of being "a glutton and a winebibber," so I'm sure that Jesus loved to eat and drink, but because His spirit was in control, He could keep His body and soul in proper balance. That's what I pray for you, and I hope you'll pray that very thing, very specifically.

Also, since the devil uses our disobedience to compound his assaults on us, may I humbly suggest that you ask your Mom's forgiveness for disobeying her when she told you not to eat so much? Of course, she'll forgive you in a second, but really it's the spiritual principle of going back to the source and removing the original cause of the problem. I believe that fear and unrest and personal dissatisfaction led to your acts of disobedience, which in turn led to all the excess weight. If you'll go right back to the beginning of that, ask your Mom's forgiveness—and very importantly, *forgive your Dad for the real anguish his actions have caused you*—you'll open the door of your spirit for God to begin miracles in and through you!

During your fasting time (which I believe should be repeated over and over until the problem is solved), ask the Lord to give you a healthy diet pattern to follow between fasts. Let me suggest several Scripture passages for spiritual bread: Romans 7 and 8; Romans 12 (the second verse talks about the renewing of your mind); First John 4 and Romans 5 (which talk about love casting out fear); Second Corinthians 11, verse 3 (shows how Satan can corrupt our mind and thought processes); and Matthew 6:31 through 33, "do not be anxious then, saying, 'What shall we eat?' or 'What shall we drink?' or, 'With what shall we clothe ourselves?' For all these things the Gentiles eagerly seek; for your Heavenly Father knows that you need all these things."

"But *seek first His kingdom*, and *His righteousness;* and all these things shall be added to you."

Dear Sandra, I know that this is a pretty sober-sounding prescription. It's not as flashy or intriguing or attractive as a water diet or a grapefruit diet or some other flesh-level solution. But this one will work! It depends on *living Water*—the power of the Holy Spirit, and works from the inside out.

God bless you—and liberate that thin, happy Sandra on the inside of you.

Yours in Christ,
PAT

6. A CURE FOR TELEVISION

Dear Pat:

Television is making me sick!

It's getting to the place where I can't let my kids watch it any night of the week, and there are very few programs that I want to watch myself. You're in the TV business; can you tell me why there's so much sex and perversion and violence on all the time? Do the networks really think we want that stuff or is it the sponsors?

It seems to me that if America isn't already down the drain, our television programming will finish us off eventually. Is there any hope?

An anxious mom,
Esther M.

Dear "Mom":

I'm eager and happy to assure you that there *is* hope for TV! I'm the guy who's still fascinated by the whole process, the incredible genius and still-unfulfilled potential of television. I can see a bright future for it as a medium, and for us as a people if we learn how to channel its power (no pun intended).

It's like atomic energy. Turned in one direction, it can destroy and wound millions but handled properly, it can benefit and bless mankind. In fact, I suspect that television has at least as much significance in our future as atomic energy—and maybe more!

Right now, though, its use is largely controlled by three men and their advisors. This can be good and it can be terrible. *It depends on who the men are, and what motivates them.* There's nothing wrong with the profit motive, if it's governed by a sense of real responsibility to the paying customer and to the public at large. You *know* that profit is the primary consideration of the three men who head up our TV networks. It has to be.

I honestly believe that these men feel a sense of responsibility to the American public, as well as to the sponsors and the owners. They have wives, children, and neighbors, and they probably belong to church groups and civic organizations just like we do. Their jobs are immensely powerful, but with that power comes tremendous pressure, uncertainty and complexity. It's one business where "you're only as good as your last rating," and the turnover at the executive level can be frighteningly swift. Along Madison Avenue in New York and in TV network offices in L.A. the ulcer count is high.

Imagine a man working his way to the top position at a major network, up from the lowly beginnings as a writer, producer or station manager, finding himself at the pinnacle of his profession with dizzying power and responsibility. He knows that if he doesn't win the ratings battles in a relatively short time, he'll be thrown down and someone else will be occupying his big office.

Would you want to be in his chair? I wouldn't.

TV affects us like almost nothing else. I would say that it wields more influence right now in American life than church, school or politics. In fact, each of those major areas is *itself* vastly influenced by TV. Ministers, teachers and politicians all spend time in front of that "magic box" and form many of their own attitudes and priorities on information dancing in that electronic crystal ball. We tend to believe what we hear and see, especially when competent voices and experienced producers prepare it for us.

TV *is* infected. It is spreading a contagious disease across America.

Violence begets violence. I don't think it's a coincidence that while blood flows freely on TV, and while terrible tragedies, murders and accidents are shown "live" on news programs, that violent crimes of all types are on a steep curve in our land.

Immorality begets immorality. As TV "mirrors" wife-swapping, promiscuity, rape, teenage sex, foul language and "alternatives" to marriage, all these things escalate dramatically.

Occult interest begets occult interest. As practically every dramatic show on TV focuses on witchcraft, demonic possession, Satanic ritual and other bizarre, twisted "religions," these things become more intriguing to the public. All over the nation these foul little groups are growing and gaining memberships, spilling into the newspapers daily as the police have to cope with the violence and sadism that results.

On and on it goes. The more we, the American public, are exposed to the worst side of human nature, the worse our own lives and attitudes are affected. It's a fact—we *are* influenced by our environment and television is a powerful part of our environment.

So what's the cure? It's so simple, so elementary, that most people won't do it.

There are two things we can all do—and they're powerful! One: *Pray for the network presidents.* Two: *Write them your feelings.*

The Bible says specifically, "I exhort therefore, that, first of all, supplications, prayers, intercessions, and giving of thanks be made for all men; for kings, and for all that are in authority; that we may lead a quiet and peaceable life in all godliness and honesty."

Notice the logic of it! Pray for those in authority over you so that *you* may lead godly and peaceful lives! Few have more authority over our lives than these three network presidents. We've tended to criticize, even curse, those men who are just trying to do what they're paid to do instead of praying *for* them, asking God to bless and encourage and influence their thinking and their motives! We've been going at it backwards, as usual.

God is just waiting for us to make Him our source, to call Him into our daily concerns, to overrule in the affairs of men. If we don't ask Him, He won't do it! If we *do*, He will! It's that simple.

And the second is important, too. Those men really want to give the American public what it desires. I believe that. The trouble is that the shows featuring bizarre, violent, and occult themes often get big ratings—indicating that the American public *wants* that stuff. Do we? Or is it simply that we'll watch a dogfight, or an accident, or a crime, if it's happening under our noses—while we'd *rather* see a Waltons or a Mary Tyler Moore or a Moses special if we were given the choice?

Well, if enough Americans write these men and let them know respectfully what our "druthers" *are*, they'll give them to us! I can promise you that. And if we'd write and *thank* them (and the sponsors) when they give us something we like, they'll see that we get more of it! It's that simple.

I've done it.

I'm enclosing a copy of a letter I've written to all three network heads. If enough of us will do a similar thing, and if we'll pray for them, things will change. It's a fact of American life, thank God, and it's a spiritual principle. I hope you'll do it, too. God bless you!

Dear _____

I'm in this crazy, wonderful, complex and exciting business of television with you. More than most of the public, I can sympathize with the pressures and problems that go with your job.

Still, as one viewer and the head of one family, I feel it's only fair to register our feelings with you about the subject matter of television today. Surely, if you really had the pulse of enough of the American people, your job would be easier. So I think we ought to let you know what we really want on television.

That marvelous flickering box sits in our living rooms, kitchens and bedrooms, and influences our children (us, too) greatly. Although there's a fascination about violence, occult things and sexual themes, and therefore their ratings are high, we're increasingly concerned about the long-range effects of a steady diet of this stuff on our national morality and attitudes.

I'm thinking now that Rembrandt and Renoir were capable of beautiful pornography and classic sadism; instead, these and other great masters chose themes that were worthy of their artistry. I beg the artists and the decision makers of television to choose themes more worthy of their talents and their positions of influence. I've long felt that talent, like water, may seek its lowest level if there are no barriers or checks to it. Regardless of the boundaries or restrictions placed upon it, true talent will always be creative. In fact, the greatest artists produce the most worthy masterpieces within the restraints of decency and morality and the inspiration of spirituality.

All I'm saying is that shows like the Waltons, Mary Tyler Moore, Lawrence Welk, Marcus Welby and Little House on the Prairie can be immensely successful, and keep people glued to those sets by the millions without a spiritual and moral and emotional fallout the next day. I know that's not the easy course; the responsible road is usually a little harder than the alternatives. But surely as we head into our bicentennial year, we should all take the time and the effort to regain some lost ground. My family and I really hope that you and the other creative people at your network will do America that great big favor. If my family and I can do anything to help, please call on us.

We're praying for you.

Warm good wishes,
Pat Boone

7. CAN WE WIN AGAINST PORNOGRAPHY?

Dear Pat,

I've got 3 children, two boys 7 and 13, and a girl 9.

It's really hard these days to raise kids with any moral sense and any convictions about right and wrong. My husband and I take them to church and Sunday school, and we take time to talk with them and answer their questions about sex and anything else.

But we can't shield them from all the twisted, unbalanced and unChristian sexual attitudes all around us. There are disgusting newspaper ads for X-rated movies, suggestive commercials on TV for R-rated films, sick porno newspapers are sold openly on the streets, and now some of this same kind of material comes to our house *in the mail!*

Isn't there anything we can do as concerned parents? I know you campaigned there in California for an anti-pornography bill but it lost, didn't it? Do people really want pornography? I'm doing the best I know to do as a parent but I feel the cards are stacked against me. I want so much for my children to have healthy, balanced, spiritual attitudes about sex but it seems I'm out of style. Any advice would sure be appreciated.

Mrs. Leonore Potter

Dear Mrs. Potter:

You really touch a nerve with me when you mention pornography!

Why the American people put up with this stuff, why we don't rise up and shake this filth off our shoulders, I can't

146

understand. I'm sure the vast majority of people in our country are as embarrassed as you and I are at the cheap advertisements, billboards, "adult" theaters, bookstores, and the streetcorner vending machines that are just the right height for little kids to gawk at.

In this, as in so many other areas of life, we keep saying, "well, maybe it won't hurt . . . ," instead of demanding and pursuing the *best*!

Abraham Lincoln said long ago that America would never be vanquished by enemies outside our borders; that if we ever fell, it would be because we lost our resolve and crumbled from within. He was right! And little by little, step by step, we're allowing the decay of immorality, compromise of ethics and the cancer of faithlessness and fear to sap us of our strength, our purpose and our identity.

We're still trying to put up a big, brave front to the world, when inside, we're becoming addicts. We're letting ourselves get "hooked" on the opiates of self-indulgence, weak-kneed permissiveness and sensual titillation.

America's getting soft, flabby, confused, indecisive, timid in character, wishy-washy, unable to distinguish between right and wrong, and so afraid of stepping on somebody's "rights" that we're surrendering our own basic freedoms.

Pornography is "exhibit A."

We've actually allowed seamy exhibitors of triple-X porno movies to use Freedom of Speech as their protective blanket. The framers of the Constitution, Tom Jefferson, Ben Franklin and the rest, would have tarred and feathered these filth-merchants and burned their wares like the disease-infested rags they are. They would be furious at *us* for allowing this mind-blurring decadence to be merchandised openly in front of our children—and especially for allowing the Constitution to protect them!

"Change it!" they would shout, *"Amend it! We pro-*vided for that; we knew you'd need to make some things more specific as the country grew. Get your congressmen and your lawyers together, state exactly what the will of the people is on this pornography question, change the wording of your laws to conform to the majority will of the people and go get the scoundrels!"

That's exactly what we tried to do here in California. Proposition 18 was drawn up by lawyers and congressmen to *define* pornography, to get unflinchingly specific about the kinds of things we, the people, don't want produced and sold in our society. Things like live sex acts, sadomasochistic sexual torture, young boys defiling themselves with old men and animals—films of children in perverted acts and depictions of human waste processes. It is hardly the kind of stuff that should be protected by the Constitution of the United States.

The proposition was defeated, 2 to 1, here in California. You see, pornography is Big Business here. 200 million dollars big!

Large law firms were hired to pick the proposition to pieces and to declare it "unconstitutional." Ad agencies were hired to mount massive publicity campaigns to convince the voters that Proposition 18 would rob them of their freedoms, that they'd not get to see LOVE STORY or PATTON, that Michelangelo's statue of David would have to be draped, that vigilante groups would be authorized to raid the public libraries and seize books and paintings according to their own perverted whims. *The top entertainers in the business were convinced by their own studios that their films and careers would suffer if the proposition passed!* They were afraid of an anti-*pornography* bill!

So these very influential entertainers made TV spots, pleading with the voters not to "give up their freedoms." The proposition was defeated.

But just a few months later the Supreme Court handed down verdicts upholding almost every basic provision of Proposition 18 and stated that local communities have the right, and *must use* it, to make and enforce their own standards of morality!

Hallelujah! So the ball is back in *your* court where it ought to be! And I can just hear Jefferson, Franklin, Paine and Hancock saying, "Get with it! Be involved! Write your congressman or *call* him! Make your will known! Get the folks in your own communities together, talk it over, show samples of this perversion to moms and dads in case they don't know what you're talking about, and select spokesmen to bombard the law enforcement and judicial offices. Flood your senators and congressmen with mail, write your newspapers, get up petitions and MAKE YOUR WILL KNOWN! YOU ARE THE PEOPLE! THE CONSTITUTION WAS DRAWN TO PROTECT *YOU*, NOT PORNOGRAPHERS!"

Yes, Mrs. Potter, you've touched a nerve with me.

I've got four lovely, unspoiled young daughters, and the prospect of being *unable* to shield their eyes and ears from man's worst depravity openly showing in newspaper ads and on the streets in front of our favorite family restaurants, makes me know that we've already lost a precious freedom—the freedom *from* pornography.

But this is America. We still have that Constitution. It will still work if we'll be as diligent as the pornographers have been.

May I recommend several sure-fire things?

First: PRAY! Most folks do that if all else fails. That's backwards. Pray first. Pray that God will intervene in the affairs of our nation, bless the efforts of those who oppose the works of darkness like pornography, and *curse* the efforts of those who promote it! He promised He'd do just that if we'd ask Him to. Read 2 Chronicles 7:14. God hates filth, sin and perversion far worse than we do—it cost the life of His own dear Son! Pray often about it.

Second: WRITE! Letters still carry a lot of weight, especially prayer-soaked ones, and in quantity. Mobilize your friends, church folks, PTA and civic clubs to write your elected representatives and tell them you've had *enough.* Start with the President, then the Senate, then the Congress, then your Governor, and on down the line to your own city and community leaders. Tell them you're just as concerned about spiritual pollution as you are about physical pollution—they'll get the message. And they can *change* things, if they know you really care.

Third: VOTE! Put men in office who will take an active interest in the spiritual well-being of your community and your neighbors. Listen to what they say, and during this next election year, let the candidates know what your concerns are and ask their positions. If you possibly can, get involved in the elective process right from the beginning. Work in the precincts, make calls for your candidate, encourage Christians to run for every office from the lowliest to the most important. Once you feel you know the best man for the job, talk to your friends and let them in on it. Tell them *why* you want him elected and that he'll work to clean up the community for you and your children. Our Bicentennial year is a great time to *be involved* in the democratic process.

Fourth: ACT! Think of your own peaceful ways to make things tough on pornographers. The Bible says, "Be not overcome with evil, but *overcome evil with good!*" For instance, several well-dressed Christian women with Bibles in their hands, standing in front of a porno book store or movie house and silently praying would greatly cut down on the trade—and who could object? And why not place some simple posters beside the vending machines that sell porno papers. We must remind passers-by of the cost of pornography to our society. Why not place a life-size cardboard cutout of a child peering into the vending machine to illustrate the final victims of this cancer?

Fifth: READ! Learn from books like *The Blueprint* and *Like a Roaring Lion,* both by George Otis, Read Scriptures like Psalm 34:14, Psalm 37:3 and 27, Luke 6:35, Hebrews

13:16, James 4:17, Galatians 5 and Philippians 4 to keep the Lord's perspective on these issues in mind. Be strengthened and motivated to "work while it is light—for the night cometh, when no man *can* work."

And again: PRAY! Bathe all this in prayer, because God does care, He will be involved with us, with our country, with our children and our government. Talk to Him, question Him, ask His guidance and intervention, commit your efforts and concerns to Him and watch how He begins to answer and *act!* Let's make that slogan on our money real again: IN GOD WE TRUST.

Pat Boone

PART SEVEN:
A GLIMPSE AT THE FUTURE

1. Pat's Letters to a Noted Astrologer on Prophecy and Astrology

1. PAT'S LETTER TO A NOTED ASTROLOGER ON PROPHECY AND ASTROLOGY

Dear Joan*

I hope this letter doesn't seem presumptuous—or worse. In a sort of roundabout way, I was approached with an invitation to introduce you at a Southern California appearance coming up soon. I don't know if the request came directly from you or not; but I've wrestled with it for a long time, nonetheless.

My wife, Shirley, and I have followed your career for some time with real interest and growing concern. Shirley talked once with our mutual friend, Dale Evans Rogers, about you and we have received very favorable impressions about your character and motivations from quite a number of people. We believe that you reverence the same God and love the same Jesus that we do. These are the key things that would tend to unite us.

But, increasingly, we are certain (based on our Bible study alone) that *there is absolutely no way to combine the service of Jesus with astrology.* Throughout the Bible, Old and New Testaments, *astrology is condemned by God and His inspired writers.* In fact, *it appears to be the world's oldest anti-God religion.*

Joan, I hope that you'll read this letter through; and more importantly, that you will read, perhaps again, the Scriptures that I've spent so much time putting together for your attention. I imagine that you've had a number of letters like this from concerned Christians, and it may be that I'm just "knocking my head against the wall"—I hope not. We

*Fictitious Name.

155

haven't met, but my only concern is for you and your service in Jesus. Yours is a great influence, and because it is, God can use you wonderfully; but so can Satan!

In the sixteenth chapter of Matthew, Jesus commends Peter for confessing with his mouth that Jesus is the Christ "the Son of the Living God." Jesus said that God had revealed that to Peter. But in the same chapter, *in less than ten verses*, Jesus said to the same man, "get thee behind me, *Satan.*" The reason Jesus made this harsh rebuke, is that He recognized the influence of Satan in this one whom He loved—and realized that if He listened to Peter, Peter's human motives (influenced by Satan) would block His divine assignment. I hope you'll read this over again in Matthew 16.

The point is, that Satan will use our best intentions and our real concern for fellow human beings against us—and against them! Therefore, Paul says in Colossians 2:8, 10, "Beware lest any man spoil you through philosophy and vain deceit, after the tradition of man, *after the rudiments of the world,* and not after *Christ.* . . . For in him dwelleth all the fulness of the Godhead bodily. And ye are complete in him, which is the head of all principality and power"!

Dear Joan, do you grasp what Jesus and Paul are saying? They are warning us so forcefully that our source for everything—guidance, revelation, example, teaching, inspiration—*everything,* must be Jesus.

God will provide everything we need, if we are looking totally to His Son and our Saviour. The instant that our human feelings and wisdom take over, we fall under the domination and into the tricks and traps of Satan. Ephesians 6:10 through 18 tells us about this struggle, in which we are all involved, especially Christians.

I guess you must have looked at some of the Scriptures which refer to astrology in the Bible. If there's any doubt in us about God's attitude toward astrology and other forms of spiritual detours, please read Isaiah 47:1 through 15; Deuteronomy 4:19; Deuteronomy 13:1 through 5; 17:2

through 7; 18:9 through 14. There are others, but these will certainly suffice to show what God's attitude is toward those who practice these things. Paul says in Ephesians 5:7 through 17 that we "as children of light" should not partake or have fellowship with "the unfruitful works of darkness, but rather reprove them."

By now, you can be furious at me. I've had a lot of letters from well-meaning people who were judging me by their understanding of the Scripture. Please believe that I'm not judging you or your motives, Joan. If the apostle Peter could come under the influence and the rebuke of Jesus, though he was operating in all good conscience, so can you and I. Please read Galatians 4:8 through 11 and James 4:4. When James uses the words "friendship of the world" as being enmity with God—the Greek word is *kosmos,* which is translated "world," or world system—it refers to the spirit system set up by Satan to deceive and delude people, well meaning or otherwise, and to entice them away from God.

I imagine you must feel somewhat defensive; after all, quite a career and a measure of national and international fame have been built upon a twin foundation in your life. If what I read is correct, including your own quotes, you are a Christian woman who also believes in, endorses and practices astrology. For you, as a Christian, to repudiate astrology and wash your hands of this Satanic trap would require the greatest amount of courage and dependence upon Jesus. Even as I write this letter, I realize that our mutual Enemy will do everything in his considerable power to prevent you from taking any such step. It would be a solar plexus blow at him and his "world system." But I pray that you will prayerfully consider doing just that.

The apostle Paul had his whole life changed by a vision; it happened on the road to Damascus (Acts 9). Describing it later in Acts 26:15 through 18, Paul says, "And I said, Who art thou, Lord? And he said, I am Jesus whom thou persecutest." Paul was not aware that he was persecuting

Jesus; he was doing all that he did in perfectly good conscience (Acts 24:16). But he *was* persecuting and opposing Jesus, and when he realized it, he stopped in his tracks and went the other way!

In Acts 26:17-18, Jesus is quoted as saying He had selected Paul to go to the Gentiles and "open their eyes, and to turn them from *darkness to light,* and *from the power of Satan unto God,* that they may receive forgiveness of sins, and inheritance among them which are *sanctified by faith that is in me."*

Our sanctification, Joan, our salvation and our only hope is in Jesus and in the God who *changes things* at the request of His believing Children. There is absolutely no hope in the stars or the planets or any kind of astrological system. To try to combine the two opposing systems is to side yourself with God's enemy and be used by him.

I'm sending along a short little readable book by Lambert Dolphin that I hope you will consider.

This has been a painful and long postponed letter. I do hope, though, that you will read and think about it—and then confer with our heavenly Father who loves you so much about whether these things are true. Jesus makes a wonderful and loving promise in the fourteenth chapter of John. That promise is for you—John 14:21 through 23. In these three sweet and powerful verses, He promises to come and reveal His will to those who really seek it and who love Him. The promise, Joan, is to you. God bless you as you think and pray and strive to serve Him faithfully.

Your humble friend,
PAT BOONE

Dear Pat:

Thank you so much for your letter. And no, it did not seem "presumptuous"! Rather, I was highly complimented that, having been invited to introduce me at my forthcoming appearance at the Hollywood Bowl, you would so painstakingly search your Christian heart and conscience and, then, so carefully and kindly explain why you felt it necessary to regret.

My husband and I have followed your career with interest and admiration. Hopefully, our present communications, however widely differing in approach, may bring us together in understanding and friendship.

Obviously, you took much time and effort to write me. I am truly grateful. I've read your letter over many times, not only because of its depth of sincerity and conviction of personal faith which prompted its utterances, but because I too have given these matters deep concern and thought. I have spent much time meditating upon their total significance and interrelationship before going ahead with and continuing my interest and work in astrology.

I have done so not only because I was taught astrology as a child by a consecrated, scholarly Jesuit priest, but because he *was* a priest, I had no reason to believe that the study of this particular subject would in any way conflict with my religious beliefs or the basic religious concepts of my Church. Indeed, the Scriptures are full of references to all the heavenly bodies and God's reasons for creating them. He tells us many times in the Bible that He created them to help His people.

The very first reference is in the beginning of Genesis: 1:16. "And God made two great lights; the greater light to rule the day, and the lesser light to rule the night: and He made the stars also."

Therefore, I learned—and it is now my premise—that God's purpose in creating the stars was so they *could be used* as guidelines by the peoples of the earth. It seems to me this is very clearly stated. The stars are God's creation and, as such, are "good," as God calls all His creations good.

You are right. The Scriptures condemn the burning of incense to idols, stars, the sun, et cetera; and soothsaying, necromancy, talismen, et cetera, in Deuteronomy and elsewhere. However, I am very careful not to fall under this condemnation by giving to the stars, the sun, or to any other creature or thing, the adoration that belongs to God alone! This would be idolatry and abhorrent to all ideas of true religious faith.

But, the Scriptures also say in Isaiah 47:13, "Thou art wearied in the multitude of thy counsels. Let now the *astrologers,* the stargazers, the monthly prognosticators, stand up, and *save thee* from these things that shall come upon thee." (Emphasis supplied.)—I know only too well that *God alone can save us* . . . not "astrologers" or "stargazers" or any other mortal.

As you say, Pat, many people are led astray if they become superstitious about looking for guidance from sources other than God, through prayer. That is why I am so careful when I study the stars that I utilize them only as a "roadmap" to support the personality of individuals to save them "from these things" that might come upon them as Isaiah so ably stated in 47:13.

You refer to the sixteenth chapter of Matthew. May I respectfully suggest that you examine chapter 2 of the Gospel. According to Saint Matthew once again, paying special attention to the story of the Three Wise Men who were led by the Star of Bethlehem to the spot where the Baby Jesus lay in the manger outside the town: "We have seen His star in the East," they said . . . and were *guided* by it to Him!

I understand they were astrologers. They followed the stars. They used them as guides when needed. But they were more than astrologers. They were transitional figures in whom the ancient beliefs of man met the Central Figure of all mankind, Jesus Christ, who was—at His Father's bidding— to bring together all men of good will in a society of justice in a world of peace.

Who knows but that all Christian history might have been changed for the worse had not those three ancient astrologers been guided by that *one star?*

From this we see that even in the Holy Scriptures a primary sort of astrology was used in man's first efforts to rise above the materialism of earth and envision his place in the heavens. History shows that astrology was the beginning of mathematics, astronomy, physical science, the reckoning of time and seasons, clocks and calendars. Should it now be condemned because some few misuse it to their own destruction? Like fire, money, science itself, astrology can be used as a medium of knowledge, help, communication; conversely, it can also be used as an instrument of vice.

Through God's mercy and wisdom, we are left free to choose!

My choice is obvious. And again, relying on the Scriptures, in Deuteronomy 18:20. "But the prophet, which shall presume to speak a word in my name, which I have not commanded him to speak, or that shall speak in the name of other gods, even *that prophet shall die.*" (Emphasis supplied.)

As I believe, so I live.

As a Christian, I do not adore, worship, or venerate the sun, moon or stars as ancient peoples did. They are "assistants" in my daily life, just as are automobiles and airplanes, pots and pans, typewriters and telephones—all joined together in harmony to help us carry out the Will of God.

As you did not judge me or my motives, so do I not judge you or yours. Rather I applaud you, for the world has need of more great Christians such as you, Pat.

Please know my prayers will be with you for your continued Divine Guidance as well as the continued success of your great works. Also, please say a little prayer for me, now and then, for like you, I have much work to do and many promises to fulfill.

Again, thank you, Pat.

Bless you always,

Joan Blank

Dear Joan:

I feel like I've come to know you already! And, Joan, as strange as this may seem, God has given me a love for you that I recognize as being from Jesus. I believe you honestly mean to serve our mutual Lord as best you know how, and so do I. What a beautiful bond this is!

Maybe, one of these days soon, the Lord intends that we sit down together, share our experiences in Him, and discuss these things more fully. Shirley and I would love to have you visit in our home while you are in Los Angeles, if this works out to your convenience.

Dear Joan, with this pure and spiritual love comes a deep concern; I pray that you can understand it and not see it as judgmental in any way. Part of the concern is that you, in your goodness and human optimism, seem to believe that there is really hope for this world and for mankind. You seem to think that man can actually be brought together and that Christianity and astrology and other philosophies and traditions can be joined in harmony as "the basis of attaining future brotherhood and peace". But all the great prophets of the Bible, *including Jesus Himself,* say this will not happen! In fact, Jesus said (Matthew 10:34) "Think not that I am come to send peace on earth: I came not to send peace, but a sword"!

Things are not going to get better and better, they're going to get worse and worse. I think you believe as I do that the coming of Jesus is not far off; a great growing number of Christian leaders all sense that the Messiah is getting ready to come and claim His own. In Luke 22:25-33 and in the whole twenty-fourth chapter of Matthew, Jesus, the great Prophet, describes the condition of the world as He poises on the very threshold of His return. In Matthew 24:7-8, He says that nations shall be pitted against nations and there will be famines and pestilences, earthquakes, and that these are just the beginning of sorrows.

In verses 12 and 13 He says that "because iniquity shall abound, the love of many shall wax cold. But He that shall endure to the end, the same shall be saved." This is hardly a picture of man united in peace and brotherhood—but it certainly is a picture of the way the world is going right now!

And finally, in that chapter, Jesus says in verses 21 and 22, "For then shall be great tribulation, such as was not since the beginning of the world to this time, no, nor ever shall be. And except those days should be shortened, there should no flesh be saved"!

None of the New Testament prophets give us any hope that the world will be in a state of sweet readiness and brotherhood when Jesus comes. In fact, Satan as a roaring lion will be turning the earth into a veritable hell. Second Timothy 3, especially verses 13 through 17 and 1 Thessalonians 5:1-5 underscore this picture. I'm no prophet, Joan, but it's easy to see that the world is hastening very quickly, prodded by Satan and all his legions, toward the climax of all history. Surely the message of the hour is Jesus' own words in Luke 21:28.

Just a couple of words about astrology: In the first place, the Bible only says that those men in the second chapter of Matthew were "wise men." It's true that they had seen a star, a very special star, but that doesn't mean that they were astrologers as we think of them today. They evidently followed that particular star for two years, and it actually moved through the heavens and stood over the spot where Jesus lay. I can't see that history would have been changed in any significant way had this not happened—but it did, and thereby fulfilled some Old Testament prophecy, and at least testified to those three men that Jesus, the Lamb of God and the Messiah, had come! God focused their attention on His Son, who in Himself would reconcile those who believe on Him to God, through the shedding of His precious blood. Paul focuses his attention on that same Jesus in Colossians 1 and 2, especially 2:6-10. Today, almost 2,000 years later, if we have Jesus dwelling in us, *we need no other guide or source.*

Dear Joan, please go back and read Isaiah 47 and 48. I fear that you have sorely missed that great prophet's message. He's talking to Babylon, and *pronouncing their doom*. I pray that you'll read both of these chapters in *The Living Bible* translation, where Kenneth Taylor does such a beautiful job of making it clear. Especially give attention to the tenth verse through the fourteenth! Isaiah underscores the helplessness of the astrologers *even to save themselves*, much less those who are depending on their advice!

Please forgive me; my letters are too long. In my concern, I may be accomplishing nothing except your irritation. If I'm way off base in even writing like this, Joan, I'm really sorry. I just feel this great sense of urgency in these days, and in my constant Bible study, I believe that the Holy Spirit is opening up the Scriptures and telling us to "get ready"! "Shout it from the housetops—Jesus is coming! Jesus is coming!" And if this is true, then the devil will try with every device at his command to lull us into false security and optimism and to distract us in every possible way from a singleminded devotion to Jesus, the Lamb of God. If people think there is *one other way* to steer clear of trouble and to chart their course through this chaotic, temptest-tossed sea of life, without having to kneel before Jesus and commit their lives to Him—they will choose that one way rather than His way. Astrology doesn't demand commitment or change; Jesus does. Jesus says, "Ye must be *born again!*"

In John 14, He says if anyone wants to know His will and His doctrine, that He and God will come and live with that person! *This* is what He's wanting to get people to understand and accept now—while there's still time!

Well, I hope this letter hasn't taken too much of your time. It's now almost a quarter to two in the morning in Seattle, and at seven I have a very important business meeting. Only Jesus could make me want to be pouring through my Bible and writing this long letter to you at this crazy hour! God bless you, dear Joan, and I want you to know that I and my family pray for you. Please pray for us, too.

Your brother in the soon coming Jesus,
PAT BOONE